Practical CockroachDB

Building Fault-Tolerant Distributed SQL Databases

Rob Reid

Apress®

Practical CockroachDB: Building Fault-Tolerant Distributed SQL Databases

Rob Reid
Liss, Hampshire, UK

ISBN-13 (pbk): 978-1-4842-8223-6   ISBN-13 (electronic): 978-1-4842-8224-3
https://doi.org/10.1007/978-1-4842-8224-3

Managing Director, Apress Media LLC: Welmoed Spahr
Acquisitions Editor: Jonathan Gennick
Development Editor: Laura Berendson
Coordinating Editor: Jill Balzano

Cover image photo by Maximalfocus on Unsplash

Distributed to the book trade worldwide by Springer Science+Business Media LLC, 1 New York Plaza, Suite 4600, New York, NY 10004. Phone 1-800-SPRINGER, fax (201) 348-4505, e-mail orders-ny@springer-sbm. com, or visit www.springeronline.com. Apress Media, LLC is a California LLC and the sole member (owner) is Springer Science + Business Media Finance Inc (SSBM Finance Inc). SSBM Finance Inc is a **Delaware** corporation.

For information on translations, please e-mail booktranslations@springernature.com; for reprint, paperback, or audio rights, please e-mail bookpermissions@springernature.com.

Apress titles may be purchased in bulk for academic, corporate, or promotional use. eBook versions and licenses are also available for most titles. For more information, reference our Print and eBook Bulk Sales web page at http://www.apress.com/bulk-sales.

Any source code or other supplementary material referenced by the author in this book is available to readers on GitHub.

Printed on acid-free paper

For Emily, Ruby, and our little one on the way.
Thank you for giving me the space and patience
I needed to put this wonderful project together.

Table of Contents

About the Author

Rob Reid is a software developer from London, England. In his career, he has written back-end, front-end, and messaging software for the police, travel, finance, commodity, sports betting, telecom, retail, and aerospace industries. He is an avid user of CockroachDB and has worked with the Cockroach Labs team in recent years to promote the database and embed it into development teams in the United States and the UK.

About the Technical Reviewer

Fernando Ipar has been working on and with open source databases since 2000, focusing on performance, scaling, and high availability. He currently works as a Database Reliability Engineer at Life360. Before that, he has worked at Perceptyx, Pythian, and Percona, among other places. When not working, Fernando enjoys going to plant nurseries with his wife and playing music with their children while being a good service employee for the family's cat.

Acknowledgments

I'm incredibly grateful to the following people. Their contributions to this book have been invaluable to me.

Kai Niemi (Solutions Engineer (EMEA) at Cockroach Labs) – I met Kai when he was a customer of Cockroach Labs and have witnessed him transition from being a CockroachDB expert at one company to an expert the global CockroachDB community can be grateful to have.

Daniel Holt (Director, Sales Engineering, International (EMEA and APAC), at Cockroach Labs) – I worked very closely with Daniel from the moment he joined Cockroach Labs and have often marvelled at his comprehensive knowledge of the database.

Katarina Vetrakova (Privacy Programme Manager at GoCardless) – Katarina is quite possibly the most enthusiastic data privacy specialist you could ever hope to meet. She's completely dedicated to the art, and since working with her at Lush, her passion and knowledge have been inspiring to me.

Jonathan Gennick (Assistant Editorial Director of Databases at Apress) – I'd like to thank Jonathan Gennick for approaching me to write this book. Without him, this amazing (and terrifying) opportunity wouldn't have found me. He has been amazing throughout the process of writing this book, and his patient knowledge sharing allowed this first-time author to really find his feet and enjoyment in writing.

The Cockroach Labs team – The Cockroach Labs team is among the smartest people I've ever met. They're incredibly dedicated to their database and its customers and are a big reason for my affection toward CockroachDB. I'd like to thank the following people from Cockroach Labs (past and present) for their help, inspiration, hospitality, and friendship: Jim Walker, Jeff Miller, Carolyn Parrish, Jordan Lewis, Bram Gruneir, Kai Niemi, Daniel Holt, Glenn Fawcett, Tim Veil, Jessica Edwards, Dan Kelly, Lakshmi Kannan, Spencer Kimball, Peter Mattis, Ben Darnell, Nate Stewart, Jesse Seldess, Andy Woods, Meagan Goldman, Megan Mueller, Andrew Deally, Isaac Wong, Vincent Giacomazza, Maria Toft, Tom Hannon, Mikael Austin, Eric Goldstein, Amruta Ranade, Armen Kopoyan, Robert Lee, Charles Sutton, Kevin Maro, James Weitzman, and anyone I've failed to mention.

Introduction

Every so often, the technology community is blessed with truly disruptive technology. We've seen the likes of Kubernetes for orchestration, Kafka for streaming, gRPC for Remote Procedure Call, and Terraform for infrastructure. CockroachDB does what these technologies have done for their respective use cases; it's a game changer for data.

I first discovered CockroachDB in 2016, where I used it to create rapid prototypes during company Hackathons at my then employer. It immediately felt familiar and as if it had been designed for a developer to build reliable and scalable software without an army of database specialists to help them.

In this book, I'll share my excitement for this database and the experience I've gained from using it for many different use cases.

Who Should Read This Book

This book is for developers, database specialists, and enterprise owners. So whether you're in a position of convincing people to use CockroachDB or you're looking for a tool to complement your enterprise tech stack, there's something in this book for you.

You don't need to have existing knowledge of CockroachDB, as we'll start with the basics and quickly ramp up to real-world examples. Any experience with relational databases (especially Postgres) will be beneficial but is not required.

Navigating This Book

This book is both an introduction and a reference to CockroachDB. It starts with the "why" of CockroachDB – why it was created and what problems it solves. It then dives into the "what" – the database's data types, constructs, and fundamentals. Finally, it covers the "how" – how you can use what you've learned to solve real-world scaling, safety, and performance challenges.

The book aims to remain practical, so it hovers above the database's internal details. To continue your journey, I recommend reading the excellent documentation and blog posts available on the Cockroach Labs website: `www.cockroachlabs.com`.

Using Code Examples

Code examples can be found in GitHub and are arranged in chapters to help you find what you're looking for as you make your way through the book.

`https://github.com/codingconcepts/practical-cockroachdb`

Code is self-contained to a chapter, meaning you won't have to read the whole book to get something working. In some cases, code examples are split across adjoining code blocks, but this will be highlighted.

I execute all of the code examples against version v21.1.7 of CockroachDB, which is the current stable version of the database at the time of writing.

Contacts

CockroachDB

info@cockroachlabs.com

53 W 23rd Street

8th Floor

New York, NY

10010

`www.cockroachlabs.com`

`https://forum.cockroachlabs.com`

Rob Reid

hello@robreid.io

`https://robreid.io`

`https://twitter.com/robreid_io`

`https://github.com/codingconcepts`

`www.linkedin.com/in/rob-reid`

CHAPTER 1

The Reason for CockroachDB

Databases are a critical part of almost every stateful system. However, correctly running them can be challenging, especially where price, availability, and shifting international data privacy regulations are concerned. CockroachDB makes navigating this tricky landscape not only easier but enjoyable.

In this chapter, we'll explore the *why* of CockroachDB – why it came to be, and why you might want to consider using it for your data.

What Is CockroachDB?

CockroachDB is a cloud-native Relational Database Management System (RDBMS). It falls into the class of "NewSQL" or "DistSQL" (Distributed SQL) databases, which aim to provide the scalability of NoSQL databases while giving users the experience and features of a traditional SQL database. It is wire-compatible with Postgres, which means you can connect to a CockroachDB cluster with most Postgres tools and drivers. To find out which drivers are available, visit `www.cockroachlabs.com/docs/stable/install-client-drivers.html`.

On paper, CockroachDB is "CP," which, in terms of the CAP Theorem, means it favors data **C**onsistency over **A**vailability in the face of network **P**artitions. In reality, however, CockroachDB – as its name suggests – has been built with availability in mind as well. In practice, if you were to lose the majority of replicas in a CockroachDB cluster, rather than compromising the integrity of your data, requests will block until the nodes have recovered. Sizing your cluster to ensure CockroachDB can continue to function in the event of lost nodes is, therefore, an essential constituent to availability.

© Rob Reid 2022
R. Reid, *Practical CockroachDB*, https://doi.org/10.1007/978-1-4842-8224-3_1

Cockroach Labs – the company behind CockroachDB – was founded in 2015 by Spencer Kimball, Peter Mattis, and Ben Darnell. Inspired by Google's Spanner database, the team sought to bring Spanner's level of scalability to the masses, removing Spanner's dependency on atomic clocks and writing in the performant, modern, and increasingly ubiquitous programming language, Go.

It gives you the freedom to create multiregion databases without the need for a database department. Importantly, it's also a safety net, making it harder to create that multiregion database incorrectly.

CockroachDB's Architecture

CockroachDB uses the Raft Consensus algorithm to give users a multiactive system, which means every node is the same. There are no special "active," "leader," or "write" nodes. Every node can receive a portion of read and write requests for different shards (or "ranges") of data, helping CockroachDB to scale horizontally.

Under the hood, CockroachDB is a distributed key/value store. But thanks to its layered architecture of SQL > Transactions > Distribution > Replication > Storage, you can interact with data as richly as you would in any other RDBMS.

What Does CockroachDB Solve?

Creating a new database is relatively easy, regardless of the technology. You download a binary, pull a Docker image, or start a subscription, and away you go. On the other hand, you typically install a traditional database on a single machine that will need to be vertically scaled, sharded, or have read replicas added when outgrown. All of these needs pose complexity, availability, and consistency challenges.

With CockroachDB, the challenges of complexity and reliability shift to the database. It takes care of distribution, scaling, and replication, leaving you to focus on your data. Generally speaking, if a cluster requires more capacity, you simply add a node to that cluster. CockroachDB will automatically rebalance the data evenly across all nodes.

Figure 1-1 depicts a cluster of three nodes, each with a capacity of 100GB and each with a 40GB share of 120GB total data.

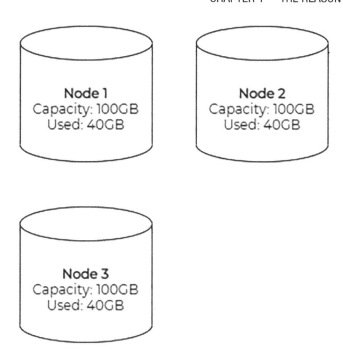

Figure 1-1. *A three-node cluster*

In Figure 1-2, you'll see that when we add a node, data in the cluster will be rebalanced across all four nodes, resulting in shares of 30GB per node of the 120GB total.

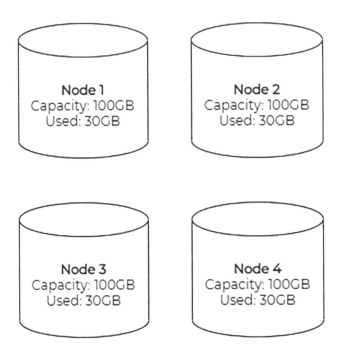

Figure 1-2. *The same cluster, rebalanced across four nodes*

Who Is CockroachDB For?

CockroachDB is an excellent choice for anyone needing a scalable, reliable, and distributed Online Transaction Processing (OLTP) database. Built with modern, cloud-based infrastructure and workloads in mind, it will be at home in the cloud, on-premises, or a hybrid of the two.

It's also a great choice if you're unsure of your database storage requirements. You can start small, expanding your cluster node by node as your data grows. CockroachDB will ensure that your data is distributed evenly and safely across the growing cluster.

If you are familiar with RDBMSs, CockroachDB will feel familiar to you. For Postgres users, you may even find that CockroachDB can be a drop-in replacement for your database.

As you'll see shortly, CockroachDB can be installed with minimal fuss whether you want to create a local development database or a distributed production database.

CockroachDB is trusted to run critical, globally distributed workflows by some of the world's largest tech, finance, travel, retail, telecoms, video streaming, and gaming companies. And its position on https://db-engines.com/en/ranking continues to improve. It is now more popular than Google's Spanner, the database that inspired it.

CHAPTER 2

Installing CockroachDB

One of CockroachDB's many strengths is the ease with which you can install it. In this chapter, we'll explore CockroachDB's licensing model and the various ways you can install it.

Licensing

We'll start with a tour of CockroachDB's licensing options to familiarize ourselves with what each option provides. There are both free and paid-for models, and your choice of model will depend on your requirements and the features available in each.

Free

There are two free options available. One is an on-premises installation of the CockroachDB Core functionality, and the other is a cloud offering:

- **CockroachDB Core** – Build and elastically scale a distributed database with many of the most critical features as standard; a good option if you don't need some of CockroachDB's more advanced features. You would need to install this option onto either cloud-based or on-premises hardware.

- **CockroachDB Serverless (Free Tier)** – Sign up and create a free CockroachDB cluster in the cloud. At the time of writing, this cloud option provides similar but slightly more limited functionality to CockroachDB Core, limiting users to a multitenant, single-node machine with 1 vCPU and 5GB of storage.

© Rob Reid 2022
R. Reid, *Practical CockroachDB*, https://doi.org/10.1007/978-1-4842-8224-3_2

Paid For

To unlock everything that CockroachDB has to offer (and to support Cockroach Labs in continuing to build the database into the future), the following paid-for models are available:

- **CockroachDB Self-Hosted** – The complete CockroachDB offering for cloud-based or on-premises installations. Sporting advanced features such as geo and archival partitioning, incremental backups, encryption at rest, change data capture, and direct support from Cockroach Labs.

- **CockroachDB Dedicated** – The complete CockroachDB offering in the cloud. In addition to CockroachDB Enterprise, it provides SLAs and cloud-specific options like VPC peering.

A decision to use any of the aforementioned licenses will depend on your requirements. In each of the following installation options, I'll provide a recap of the licensing model to help you decide which best matches your needs.

CockroachDB Core

Beginning in version 19.2, CockroachDB Core is subject to multiple licenses. Some functionality retains the original Apache 2.0 license, meaning it is fully Open Source. Other features are subject to a Cockroach Community License, which protects Cockroach Labs from companies using their code to build products that do not benefit Cockroach Labs.

In short, if you plan on using CockroachDB Core's free features to power your own databases and do not intend to sell CockroachDB as a service to others, CockroachDB Core is a good choice for you.

Local Installation

In this section, I'll show you how to install CockroachDB on your local machine. For each installation method, we'll run CockroachDB with insecure configuration for brevity for each installation method, which means **no authentication or encryption**. This is acceptable for a local development database but not for anything else. Once we've installed and tested local insecure deployments, we'll move on to some real-world secure implementations.

Binary Install

You can install the `cockroach` binary in several ways, depending on your operating system.

For Linux users, run the following commands to get started:

```
$ curl https://binaries.cockroachdb.com/cockroach-v21.1.7.linux-amd64.tgz
| tar -xz

$ sudo cp cockroach-v21.1.7.linux-amd64/cockroach /usr/local/bin/
```

For Mac users, run the following command to get started:

```
$ brew install cockroachdb/tap/cockroach
```

For Windows 10 users, run the following commands to get started:

```
$ curl -o cockroach-v21.1.7.windows-6.2-amd64.zip
https://binaries.cockroachdb.com/cockroach-v21.1.7.windows-6.2-amd64.zip

$ powershell.exe -NoP -NonI -Command "Expand-Archive '.\cockroach-
v21.1.7.windows-6.2-amd64.zip' '.'"
```

Either change directory (`cd`) into the `cockroach-v21.1.7.windows-6.2-amd64` directory and invoke the `cockroach` executable when you need it, or add its containing directory to your PATH and invoke the `cockroach` executable from any directory.

The `cockroach` executable is now available, and you can start a local instance of CockroachDB using the following command:

```
$ cockroach start-single-node --insecure --listen-addr=localhost
```

We've just started a single node, insecure cluster, listening on localhost with the default 26527 port for SQL connections and the 8080 port for HTTP connections.

To test that CockroachDB is up and running, use the `cockroach sql` command to enter the CockroachDB SQL shell. Note that the `--host` argument can be omitted, as the default value assumes a locally running node using the default port:

```
$ cockroach sql --insecure
#
# Welcome to the CockroachDB SQL shell.
# All statements must be terminated by a semicolon.
```

```
# To exit, type: \q.
#
# Client version: CockroachDB CCL v21.1.5 (x86_64-w64-mingw32, built
2021/07/02 04:03:50, go1.15.11)
# Server version: CockroachDB CCL v21.1.7 (x86_64-w64-mingw32, built
2021/08/09 18:01:51, go1.15.14)
# Cluster ID: 66424e6d-680e-4b26-8d8f-e029967b00c4
#
# Enter \? for a brief introduction.
#
root@:26257/defaultdb>
```

Docker Install

To install CockroachDB with Docker, first, make sure you have Docker installed on your machine. If you don't have Docker installed, visit the Docker installation website https://docs.docker.com/get-docker for instructions.

You can start an instance of CockroachDB in Docker with the following command:

```
$ docker run \
    --rm -it \
    --name=cockroach \
    -p 26257:26257 \
    -p 8080:8080 \
    cockroachdb/cockroach:v21.1.7 start-single-node \
        --insecure
```

This command will pull the CockroachDB Docker image and run it with port 26257 for client connections and port 8080 for HTTP connections exposed. The command will block until the process terminates, at which point, the CockroachDB Docker container will be stopped and removed.

To test that CockroachDB is up and running, use the cockroach sql command to enter the CockroachDB SQL shell:

```
$ cockroach sql --insecure
#
# Welcome to the CockroachDB SQL shell.
```

```
# All statements must be terminated by a semicolon.
# To exit, type: \q.
#
# Client version: CockroachDB CCL v21.1.5 (x86_64-w64-mingw32, built
2021/07/02 04:03:50, go1.15.11)
# Server version: CockroachDB CCL v21.1.7 (x86_64-unknown-linux-gnu, built
2021/08/09 17:55:28, go1.15.14)
# Cluster ID: 0b3ff09c-7bcc-4631-8121-335cfd83b04c
#
# Enter \? for a brief introduction.
#
root@:26257/defaultdb>
```

Kubernetes Install

To install CockroachDB with Kubernetes, make sure you have the following prerequisites installed:

- **A local installation of Kubernetes** – There are plenty of ways you can install Kubernetes on your machine. Here are some of the options available:

  - kind
    (https://kind.sigs.k8s.io/docs/user/quick-start)

  - minikube
    (https://minikube.sigs.k8s.io/docs/start)

  - k3s
    (https://rancher.com/docs/k3s/latest/en/installation)

  I will be using kind to create a local Kubernetes cluster, and at the time of writing, this installs Kubernetes version 1.21.

- **kubectl** – The Kubernetes CLI; visit
  https://kubernetes.io/docs/tasks/tools for installation instructions.

With these prerequisites installed, we're ready to get started.

Being a database, CockroachDB is considered a stateful resource in Kubernetes, so you'll need to give it a Persistent Volume Claim (PVC). PVCs live at the node level, not at the pod level, so your data will be safe if any of your CockroachDB pods get deleted or restarted.

To install a simple CockroachDB cluster in Kubernetes, create the files described in each of the following subsections. If you'd rather avoid handcrafting the following files, you can apply a ready-made Kubernetes manifest from Cockroach Labs here:

https://github.com/cockroachdb/cockroach/blob/master/cloud/kubernetes/
cockroachdb-statefulset.yaml

1_pod-disruption-budget.yaml

This file creates the PodDisruptionBudget resource for our StatefulSet. A Pod Disruption Budget provides Kubernetes with a tolerance for pod failures against a given application (identified by the selector "cockroachdb"). It ensures that there are never more than maxUnavailable pods unavailable in the cluster at any one time. By setting this to 1, we'll prevent Kubernetes from removing more than 1 CockroachDB node during operations like rolling updates, etc.

If you're configuring a cluster of 5 nodes in Kubernetes, consider setting this to 2, as you'll still have a 3-node cluster if 2 of your nodes are temporarily unavailable.

```
apiVersion: policy/v1
kind: PodDisruptionBudget
metadata:
  name: cockroachdb-budget
  labels:
    app: cockroachdb
spec:
  selector:
    matchLabels:
      app: cockroachdb
  maxUnavailable: 1
```

Run the following command to create the pod disruption budget:

```
$ kubectl apply -f 1_pod-disruption-budget.yaml
```

2_stateful-set.yaml

Now we're getting into the guts of our Kubernetes configuration. It's time to create our StatefulSet. A StatefulSet is like a deployment that provides additional guarantees around pod scheduling to ensure that pods have a persistent disk.

```yaml
apiVersion: apps/v1
kind: StatefulSet
metadata:
  name: cockroachdb
spec:
  serviceName: "cockroachdb"
  replicas: 3
  selector:
    matchLabels:
      app: cockroachdb
  template:
    metadata:
      labels:
        app: cockroachdb
    spec:
      affinity:
        podAntiAffinity:
          preferredDuringSchedulingIgnoredDuringExecution:
          - weight: 1
            podAffinityTerm:
              labelSelector:
                matchExpressions:
                - key: app
                  operator: In
                  values:
                  - cockroachdb
              topologyKey: kubernetes.io/hostname
      containers:
      - name: cockroachdb
        image: cockroachdb/cockroach:v21.1.7
```

```yaml
      imagePullPolicy: IfNotPresent
      resources:
        requests:
          cpu: "1"
          memory: "1Gi"
        limits:
          cpu: "1"
          memory: "1Gi"
      ports:
      - containerPort: 26257
        name: grpc
      - containerPort: 8080
        name: http
      readinessProbe:
        httpGet:
          path: "/health?ready=1"
          port: http
        initialDelaySeconds: 10
        periodSeconds: 5
        failureThreshold: 2
      volumeMounts:
      - name: datadir
        mountPath: /cockroach/cockroach-data
      env:
      - name: COCKROACH_CHANNEL
        value: kubernetes-insecure
      - name: GOMAXPROCS
        valueFrom:
          resourceFieldRef:
            resource: limits.cpu
            divisor: "1"
      command:
        - "/bin/bash"
        - "-ecx"
        - exec
```

```
            /cockroach/cockroach
            start
            --logtostderr
            --insecure
            --advertise-host $(hostname -f)
            --http-addr 0.0.0.0
            --join cockroachdb-0.cockroachdb,cockroachdb-1.
              cockroachdb,cockroachdb-2.cockroachdb
            --cache 25%
            --max-sql-memory 25%
      terminationGracePeriodSeconds: 60
      volumes:
      - name: datadir
        persistentVolumeClaim:
          claimName: datadir
  podManagementPolicy: Parallel
  updateStrategy:
    type: RollingUpdate
  volumeClaimTemplates:
  - metadata:
      name: datadir
    spec:
      accessModes:
        - "ReadWriteOnce"
      resources:
        requests:
          storage: 1Gi
```

Run the following command to create the stateful set:

```
$ kubectl apply -f 2_stateful-set.yaml
```

Whether you're a seasoned Kubernetes user or not, a lot is going on here. I'll take you through some of the less obvious configuration blocks to further demystify the configuration.

```
podAntiAffinity:
  preferredDuringSchedulingIgnoredDuringExecution:
  - weight: 1
    podAffinityTerm:
      labelSelector:
        matchExpressions:
        - key: app
          operator: In
          values:
          - cockroachdb
      topologyKey: kubernetes.io/hostname
```

You can ask the Kubernetes scheduler to give pods an affinity or an antiaffinity to other pods. By doing this, you're either asking them to be placed together or placed away from one another, respectively.

To highlight the importance of this configuration, let's assume that our Kubernetes cluster is running in the cloud and each node is running in a different availability zone (AZ). This podAntiAffinity rule asks Kubernetes to launch each cockroachdb pod on a different node (identified by its kubernetes. io/hostname"). Depending on your requirements, you may prefer to use the requiredDuringSchedulingIgnoredDuringExecution rule, which guarantees that each pod schedules onto a different node. This makes sense for clusters with multiple Kubernetes nodes but not for our local, single-node Kubernetes cluster.

```
env:
- name: COCKROACH_CHANNEL
  value: kubernetes-insecure
- name: GOMAXPROCS
  valueFrom:
    resourceFieldRef:
      resource: limits.cpu
      divisor: "1"
```

In this block, we're setting the environment variables consumed during both initialization and runtime. The COCKROACH_CHANNEL variable will help us identify how we installed the cluster (e.g., installed securely on Kubernetes or installed via helm, etc.). The GOMAXPROCS variable is passed to CockroachDB and used by the Go runtime to limit the CPU cores allocated to the CockroachDB process.

```
command:
  - "/bin/bash"
  - "-ecx"
  - exec
    /cockroach/cockroach
    start
        --logtostderr
        --insecure
    --advertise-host $(hostname -f)
    --http-addr 0.0.0.0
    --join cockroachdb-0.cockroachdb,cockroachdb-1.
cockroachdb,cockroachdb-2.cockroachdb
    --cache 25%
    --max-sql-memory 25%
```

In this block, we're passing some arguments to the CockroachDB executable. These arguments tell CockroachDB how to discover other nodes and how to be discovered *by* other nodes and set memory constraints for the database. These are useful when running on machines where resources are limited.

```
volumeClaimTemplates:
- metadata:
    name: datadir
  spec:
    accessModes:
      - "ReadWriteOnce"
    resources:
      requests:
        storage: 1Gi
```

In this block, we're asking Kubernetes for 1 gibibyte[1] of disk storage. There are various access modes available, but I'm using ReadWriteOnce as we only need to allocate disk space for each node once.

---

[1] 1 gibibyte = 2^{30} = 1,073,741,824 bytes

3_private-service.yaml

This file creates the Kubernetes service that will be used both by the CockroachDB nodes to discover one another and by other resources in the Kubernetes cluster. It will not be available outside of the cluster, as it doesn't expose a cluster IP.

Exposing port 26257 will allow the CockroachDB nodes to communicate with one another, and exporting port 8080 will allow services like Terraform to obtain metrics.

```
apiVersion: v1
kind: Service
metadata:
  name: cockroachdb
  labels:
    app: cockroachdb
spec:
  ports:
  - name: tcp
    port: 26257
    targetPort: 26257
  - name: http
    port: 8080
    targetPort: 8080
  publishNotReadyAddresses: true
  clusterIP: None
  selector:
    app: cockroachdb
```

Run the following command to create the private service:

```
$ kubectl apply -f 3_private-service.yaml
```

4_public-service.yaml

This file creates a Kubernetes LoadBalancer Service that will be used for external connections to the CockroachDB nodes. We'll use this service to connect to the database later.

> **Warning**   Depending on your infrastructure, when running a hosted instance of Kubernetes, a `LoadBalancer` service may create a publicly accessible endpoint. Consider creating an internal load balancer or using a ClusterIP service and making the service available via a hardened ingress.

Exposing port 26257 will allow us to connect to the database, and exposing port 8080 will allow us to view its dashboard. The following code creates a Kubernetes service that exposes the ports defined in the StatefulSet.

```yaml
apiVersion: v1
kind: Service
metadata:
  name: cockroachdb-public
  labels:
    app: cockroachdb
spec:
  ports:
  - name: tcp
    port: 26257
    targetPort: 26257
  - name: http
    port: 8080
    targetPort: 8080
  selector:
    app: cockroachdb
  type: LoadBalancer
```

Run the following command to create the private service:

```
$ kubectl apply -f 4_public-service.yaml
```

5_init.yaml

This file initializes the CockroachDB cluster. When run, it will connect to the first node in the cluster to perform initialization. In our case, we could have specified any of the nodes to start the initialization, as they are all configured to connect to the other nodes via the `--join` argument.

```yaml
apiVersion: batch/v1
kind: Job
metadata:
  name: init
  labels:
    app: cockroachdb
spec:
  template:
    spec:
      containers:
      - name: init
        image: cockroachdb/cockroach:v21.1.7
        imagePullPolicy: IfNotPresent
        command:
          - "/cockroach/cockroach"
          - "init"
          - "--insecure"
          - "--host=cockroachdb-0.cockroachdb"
      restartPolicy: Never
```

Run the following command to create the initialization job:

```
$ kubectl apply -f 5_init.yaml
```

If you've got to this point, you'll have a working CockroachDB cluster running in Kubernetes! There are a lot of moving parts in this example, so your mileage may vary. If your local Kubernetes cluster is running in Docker and you're experiencing issues, make sure that you've given Docker enough memory to run this example. 6GB should be plenty.

To connect to the cluster's HTTP endpoint, create a port-forward to the public service and open http://localhost:8080:

```
$ kubectl port-forward service/cockroachdb-public 8080
Forwarding from 127.0.0.1:8080 -> 8080
Forwarding from [::1]:8080 -> 8080
```

To connect to the cluster's SQL endpoint, create a port-forward to the public service:

```
$ kubectl port-forward service/cockroachdb-public 26257
Forwarding from 127.0.0.1:26257 -> 26257
Forwarding from [::1]:26257 -> 26257
```

Then use the cockroach command as if your cluster was running locally:

```
$ cockroach sql --insecure
#
# Welcome to the CockroachDB SQL shell.
# All statements must be terminated by a semicolon.
# To exit, type: \q.
#
# Server version: CockroachDB CCL v21.1.7 (x86_64-unknown-linux-gnu, built
2021/08/09 17:55:28, go1.15.14) (same version as client)
# Cluster ID: c3f571a3-1f67-44ab-9a62-d6f3ce6a6b20
#
# Enter \? for a brief introduction.
#
root@:26257/defaultdb>
```

If you'd rather connect to the CockroachDB cluster from *within* Kubernetes, run the following command to create a Kubernetes pod that opens a SQL shell:

```
$ kubectl run cockroachdb --rm -it \
    --image=cockroachdb/cockroach:v21.1.7 \
    --restart=Never \
    -- sql \
        --insecure \
        --host=cockroachdb-public
#
# Enter \? for a brief introduction.
#
root@cockroachdb-public:26257/defaultdb>
```

Multinode Clusters

Up to this point, we've only created single-node, local clusters, which are not advised for real-world use cases, as such clusters cannot provide resilience. Instead, it's better to create clusters of at least three nodes to survive a failure of one node, or at least five nodes to survive a failure of two nodes.

The CockroachDB documentation provides guidance on the topologies you'll need to use in order to survive everything from single-node to multiregion failures: `www.cockroachlabs.com/docs/stable/disaster-recovery.html`

There are plenty of ways to install a multinode CockroachDB cluster. A Kubernetes StatefulSet deployment is one of the more accessible options. It takes care of the manual work involved in managing multiple application instances such as service discovery and rolling updates. In the previous section on installing via Kubernetes, had we been working with a multinode/region cluster, our StatefulSet would have deployed one CockroachDB node to each of them.

In this section, we'll simulate a three-node CockroachDB cluster with the cockroach binary.

First, start the three nodes with the following commands:

```
$ cockroach start \
  --insecure \
  --store=node1 \
  --listen-addr=localhost:26257 \
  --http-addr=localhost:8080 \
  --join=localhost:26257,localhost:26258,localhost:26259

$ cockroach start \
  --insecure \
  --store=node2 \
  --listen-addr=localhost:26258 \
  --http-addr=localhost:8081 \
  --join=localhost:26257,localhost:26258,localhost:26259

$ cockroach start \
  --insecure \
  --store=node3 \
  --listen-addr=localhost:26259 \
```

```
--http-addr=localhost:8082 \
--join=localhost:26257,localhost:26258,localhost:26259
```

Next, initialize the cluster by executing the `init` command against one of the nodes:

```
$ cockroach init --insecure --host=localhost:26257
Cluster successfully initialized
```

Finally, connect to the cluster by executing the `sql` command against one of the nodes:

```
$ cockroach sql --insecure --host=localhost:26257
#
# Welcome to the CockroachDB SQL shell.
# All statements must be terminated by a semicolon.
# To exit, type: \q.
#
# Server version: CockroachDB CCL v21.1.7 (x86_64-apple-darwin19, built
2021/08/09 17:58:36, go1.15.14) (same version as client)
# Cluster ID: 689b7704-af5d-4527-a638-bad622fff923
#
# Enter \? for a brief introduction.
#
root@localhost:26257/defaultdb>
```

If you're creating a cluster on a known set of machines and you'd rather avoid orchestration tools like Kubernetes, this might be a good option for you.

Multiregion Clusters

For many use cases, installing CockroachDB into multiple availability zones (AZs) within a cloud provider region will provide a suitable level of resilience for your database.

If you require more resiliency than a single-region deployment can provide, CockroachDB has you covered again. In this section, we'll simulate a multiregion deployment using the `cockroachdb` binary. This cluster will survive not only AZ failures but also complete cloud provider *region* failures.

Multiregion Deployment

In the previous example, we were operating *within* a cloud provider region. A single AZ failure would have removed one CockroachDB node from the cluster, leaving two nodes to continue working until it was available again. From a latency perspective, this would have been acceptable, thanks to the proximity of the other nodes.

On a map, our cluster may have looked similar to the cluster in Figure 2-1. Note that the map view for nodes is only available for Enterprise clusters:

Figure 2-1. *Single-region, multinode cluster*

All nodes are located within a given cloud provider region (e.g., us-east1, as shown previously).

In the following example, we're operating *across* cloud provider regions. This means the distance (and latency) between regions may be significant. Creating a cluster with one node in each region would therefore be a bad idea. Consider Figure 2-2, where we've taken our three-node, single-region cluster and have installed it across regions instead of AZs. If we lose one node, the cluster will continue to work with two. However, as mentioned, the latency between nodes will now be much greater.

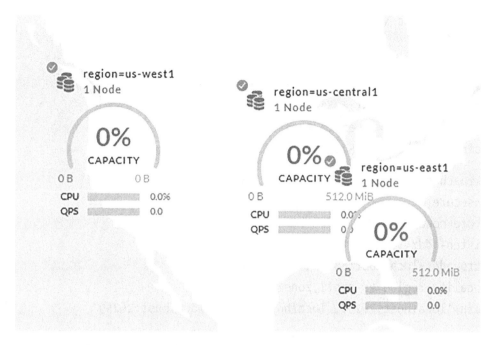

Figure 2-2. *Multiregion, single-node cluster*

Outages aside, our cluster will be spending a lot of time replicating data between nodes. When writing to CockroachDB in a three-node replicated cluster, consensus between the leaseholder node (the primary write node for a range of data) and at least one of its follower nodes will need to be achieved. This will take time in a cross-region cluster, making writes very slow.

We need a new topology.

In this example, we'll partition our data by region so that database consumers (users and applications, etc.) will access their closest region for all write operations. For a cluster like this to provide adequate regional and zonal resilience, we'll now need nine nodes. Use the following commands to create these:

```
$ cockroach start \
  --insecure \
  --store=node1 \
  --listen-addr=localhost:26257 \
  --http-addr=localhost:8080 \
  --locality=region=us-east1,zone=us-east1a \
  --join='localhost:26257, localhost:26258, localhost:26259'
```

```
$ cockroach start \
  --insecure \
  --store=node2 \
  --listen-addr=localhost:26258 \
  --http-addr=localhost:8081 \
  --locality=region=us-east1,zone=us-east1b \
  --join='localhost:26257, localhost:26258, localhost:26259'

$ cockroach start \
  --insecure \
  --store=node3 \
  --listen-addr=localhost:26259 \
  --http-addr=localhost:8082 \
  --locality=region=us-east1,zone=us-east1c \
  --join='localhost:26257, localhost:26258, localhost:26259'

$ cockroach start \
  --insecure \
  --store=node4 \
  --listen-addr=localhost:26260 \
  --http-addr=localhost:8083 \
  --locality=region=us-central1,zone=us-central1a \
  --join='localhost:26257, localhost:26258, localhost:26259'

$ cockroach start \
  --insecure \
  --store=node5 \
  --listen-addr=localhost:26261 \
  --http-addr=localhost:8084 \
  --locality=region=us-central1,zone=us-central1b \
  --join='localhost:26257, localhost:26258, localhost:26259'

$ cockroach start \
  --insecure \
  --store=node6 \
  --listen-addr=localhost:26262 \
  --http-addr=localhost:8085 \
```

```
  --locality=region=us-central1,zone=us-central1c \
  --join='localhost:26257, localhost:26258, localhost:26259'

$ cockroach start \
  --insecure \
  --store=node7 \
  --listen-addr=localhost:26263 \
  --http-addr=localhost:8086 \
  --locality=region=us-west1,zone=us-west1a \
  --join='localhost:26257, localhost:26258, localhost:26259'

$ cockroach start \
  --insecure \
  --store=node8 \
  --listen-addr=localhost:26264 \
  --http-addr=localhost:8087 \
  --locality=region=us-west1,zone=us-west1b \
  --join='localhost:26257, localhost:26258, localhost:26259'

$ cockroach start \
  --insecure \
  --store=node9 \
  --listen-addr=localhost:26265 \
  --http-addr=localhost:8088 \
  --locality=region=us-west1,zone=us-west1c \
  --join='localhost:26257, localhost:26258, localhost:26259'
```

Next, initialize the cluster by executing the init command against one of the nodes:

```
$ cockroach init --insecure --host=localhost:26257
Cluster successfully initialized
```

To partition the database in this way, we'll need an Enterprise license. You can obtain a free 30-day trial license from the Cockroach Labs website. Visit the www.cockroachlabs.com/get-cockroachdb/enterprise/ page and grab your trial Enterprise license now.

It's time to convert the cluster to Enterprise! Connect to one of the nodes in the cluster and run the following commands, substituting the `cluster.organization` and `enterprise.license` values with the ones you received in the Enterprise trial email:

```
$ cockroach sql --insecure --host=localhost:26257
#
# Welcome to the CockroachDB SQL shell.
# All statements must be terminated by a semicolon.
# To exit, type: \q.
#
# Server version: CockroachDB CCL v21.1.7 (x86_64-apple-darwin19, built
2021/08/09 17:58:36, go1.15.14) (same version as client)
# Cluster ID: 689b7704-af5d-4527-a638-bad622fff923
#
# Enter \? for a brief introduction.
#
root@localhost:26257/defaultdb> SET CLUSTER SETTING cluster.organization =
'YOUR_ORGANISATION';
SET CLUSTER SETTING

root@localhost:26257/defaultdb> SET CLUSTER SETTING enterprise.license =
'YOUR_ENTERPRISE_LICENSE';
SET CLUSTER SETTING
```

Visit the Cluster Console for one of the nodes in the cluster (e.g., `http://localhost:8080`) and switch the Node List to Node Map. Figure 2-3 shows what you'll see with an Enterprise Cluster in the Cluster Map view this time.

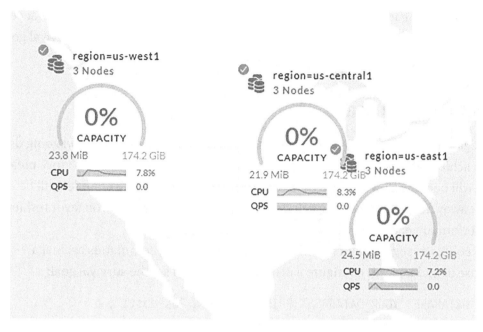

Figure 2-3. *Multiregion, multinode cluster*

CockroachDB allows you to decide how the cluster should behave in the event of zonal or regional failure. These are configured as "Survival Goals" options, and your decision of which one to use should be based on your resilience and performance requirements.

Zone Failure Goal

The Zone Failure Goal (CockroachDB's default setting) provides resilience against a cloud provider *zone* going down within a region. If two zones go down in the same region, your cluster is not guaranteed to function correctly. If you favor performance over resilience, this might be a good option for you.

To configure zone failure resilience, run the following command against a database to configure a primary region and set the survival goal:

```
ALTER DATABASE "YOUR_DATABASE" PRIMARY REGION "us-east1";
ALTER DATABASE "YOUR_DATABASE" SURVIVE ZONE FAILURE;
```

By running the following command, we'll see that the number of replicas is set to 3, the default value for CockroachDB with or without explicitly configuring survival goals.

```
SHOW ZONE CONFIGURATION FROM RANGE default;
```

Regional Failure Goal

The Region Failure Goal provides resilience against a cloud provider *region* going down. This is achieved by increasing the replication factor of the database from 3 to 5, meaning writes will become slower in the event of a region outage, as follower nodes will be further away from the leaseholder node until the region recovers. If you favor resilience over performance, this might be a good option for you.

To configure region failure resilience, run the following commands against a database to add regions, configure a primary region, and set the survival goal:

```
ALTER DATABASE "YOUR_DATABASE" PRIMARY REGION "us-east1";
ALTER DATABASE "YOUR_DATABASE" ADD REGION "us-west1";
ALTER DATABASE "YOUR_DATABASE" ADD REGION "us-central1";
ALTER DATABASE "YOUR_DATABASE" SURVIVE REGION FAILURE;
```

This database is now configured to survive region failures instead of zone failures. Now run the following command to set the number of replicas to 5.

```
SHOW ZONE CONFIGURATION FROM DATABASE defaultdb;
```

The demo Command

The cockroach CLI's demo command starts an in-memory CockroachDB Enterprise cluster on your machine. The Enterprise license for this cluster is valid for one hour, which is plenty of time to try out CockroachDB's enterprise features. Once expired, you simply rerun the demo command to start another hour.

We'll run a local CockroachDB Enterprise cluster via the demo command for most examples in this book. Any CockroachDB Enterprise features demonstrated will be clearly highlighted.

CockroachDB Serverless/Dedicated

If you prefer to use Software-as-a-Service (SaaS) tools, CockroachDB Serverless and CockroachDB Dedicated (collectively referred to as "CockroachDB Serverless") are a great way to get started with CockroachDB. Both services allow you to spin up a secure CockroachDB cluster in a matter of seconds. Depending on your requirements, it provides everything from free single-core/5GB/multitenant instances of CockroachDB to multiregion Enterprise clusters hosted on your choice of cloud provider.

Creating a Cluster

Let's create and connect to a free-tier CockroachDB Serverless instance now.

First, head to `https://cockroachlabs.cloud` and register for an account if you don't already have one. Cockroach Labs will not ask for you any billing information.

Next, choose the Free plan, select your preferred cloud provider, choose a deployment region, provide a name, and create your cluster. At the time of writing, you can choose to host your Free Tier instance in either GCP's europe-west1, us-central1, and asia-southeast1 regions or AWS's eu-west-1, us-west-2, and ap-southeast-1 regions.

After approximately 20 seconds, your cluster will be ready for connections.

Connecting to Your Cluster

To connect to your cluster from the command line, download the root certificate for your cluster. To do this, run the following command, replacing the emboldened text with your cluster ID. This will be a UUID that forms part of the URL path when visiting the cluster via the CockroachDB Serverless site:

```
$ curl -o root.crt https://cockroachlabs.cloud/clusters/YOUR_
CLUSTER_ID/cert
```

Next, connect to your database via the SQL shell using the following command. The emboldened text will be provided by the UI when you click on Connect:

```
$ cockroach sql --url 'postgresql://YOUR_USERNAME:YOUR_PASSWORD@free-
tier5.gcp-europe-west1.cockroachlabs.cloud:26257/defaultdb?sslmode=verify-
full&sslrootcert=root.crt&options=--cluster=YOUR_CLUSTER_NAME'
```

Summary

In this chapter, we've covered a lot of ground. Let's recap on the things we've learned:

- **Licensing options** – There are several licensing options available for CockroachDB. CockroachDB Enterprise provides features like geo-partitioning that are not available in CockroachDB Core, so you must choose the right license for your requirements.

- **Local installation** – We've installed CockroachDB locally with the `cockroach` binary, the Docker image, and Kubernetes. Each provides benefits depending on your stage of development. We've also looked into multinode and multiregion clusters, scenarios that will become important as your CockroachDB infrastructure matures.

- **CockroachDB as a Service** – We've created a simple Free Tier CockroachDB cluster using CockroachDB Serverless, which gives us a 5GB database to experiment with CockroachDB.

CHAPTER 3

Concepts

It's time to dive deeper into CockroachDB! This chapter explores some of CockroachDB's building blocks, including data types, indexes, and geo-partitioning.

First, let's explore the top-level objects that make up CockroachDB.

Database Objects

As Figure 3-1 shows, objects in CockroachDB are arranged hierarchically.

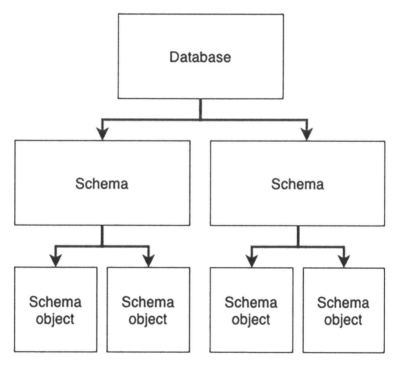

Figure 3-1. *CockroachDB object hierarchy*

© Rob Reid 2022
R. Reid, *Practical CockroachDB*, https://doi.org/10.1007/978-1-4842-8224-3_3

At the top level of the CockroachDB object hierarchy, there are databases. Databases contain schemas that, in turn, contain schema objects like tables and views.

Every CockroachDB cluster will contain the following three databases when it starts:

- **defaultdb** – The defaultdb database that clients will connect to if they don't provide a database name in their connection configuration. This database is empty and does not provide any contextual information to the schema objects contained within it. For that reason, it's best to avoid using this database and prefer to create and reference named databases explicitly. If you don't need this database, you can delete it.

- **postgres** – The postgres database exists to provide compatibility with Postgres clients. If you don't need this database, you can delete it.

- **system** – The system database provides core information to the CockroachDB cluster, including information relating to jobs, ranges, replication, geo-locations, users, and more.

In every database, there are schemas. Schemas are CockroachDB's second-level object. They allow you to separate objects like tables and views into logical areas. Say, for example, you have two business areas, each needing their own tables; having a schema per business area not only keeps those tables logically separated but also resolves naming collisions. Having two tables named "employee," for example, would not be possible within the same schema. With two schemas, this is not an issue.

The following default schemas (or "System Catalogs") exist for all new databases:

```
root@:26257/blah> show schemas;
     schema_name     | owner
---------------------+--------
  crdb_internal      | NULL
  information_schema | NULL
  pg_catalog         | NULL
  pg_extension       | NULL
  public             | admin
```

- **crdb_internal** – The crdb_internal schema contains information relating to the internal objects used by a database. This includes things like metrics, jobs, alerts, leases, and audit entries for CREATE operations.

- **information_schema** – The information_schema schema contains information on user-defined objects such as columns, indexes, tables, and views.

- **pg_catalog** – The pg_catalog schema provides compatibility with Postgres clients that are expecting a schema with this name to exist. It contains information relating to databases and the objects they contain.

- **pg_extension** – The pg_extension schema provides extension information. By default, this includes information from the Spatial Features extension, which provides spatial data types.

- **public** – In the same way that the defaultdb database is used if no database name is provided, the public schema is the default schema that is used if no user-defined schema is provided. All user-defined objects go into this schema unless the user provides another.

Underneath schemas are CockroachDB's third and final-level objects. These include indexes, sequences, tables, views, and temporary objects (objects like temporary tables that are not persisted).

Data Types

CockroachDB boasts all of the data types you'll need to build a rich database. In this section, I'll show you how and where to use these data types.

UUID

The UUID data type stores a 128-bit UUID value. Values stored in this column can be any UUID version[1] but will all be formatted using RFC 4122 standards. Let's create a table with a UUID column to learn more about it.

First, let's create a contrived table that includes a UUID column:

```
CREATE TABLE person (id UUID);
```

---

[1] https://en.wikipedia.org/wiki/Universally_unique_identifier

Next, we'll insert some data into it; note that UUIDs are valid with or without curly braces, as Uniform Resource Names (URNs), or as 16-byte strings:

```
INSERT INTO person (id) VALUES ('a33c928b-a138-4419-9f1f-8d8a137235d3');
INSERT INTO person (id) VALUES ('{1800ebff-bf6d-52c0-842f-d8db25e15ced}');
INSERT INTO person (id) VALUES ('urn:uuid:f2c6408a-3c3f-4071-9bcf-1a669d
40c07f');
INSERT INTO person (id) VALUES (b'1oqpb0zna$*k4al~');
```

Selecting the UUIDs out of the table reveals their stored representation, even though we inserted them differently:

```
SELECT * FROM person;
                    id
----------------------------------------
  a33c928b-a138-4419-9f1f-8d8a137235d3
  1800ebff-bf6d-52c0-842f-d8db25e15ced
  f2c6408a-3c3f-4071-9bcf-1a669d40c07f
  316f7170-6230-7a6e-6124-2a6b34616c7e
```

UUID columns are a great choice when you need unique IDs for tables. Rather than providing the UUIDs ourselves, let's ask CockroachDB to generate them for us on-insert:

```
CREATE TABLE "person" (
    "id" UUID DEFAULT gen_random_uuid() PRIMARY KEY
);
```

CockroachDB will only generate a default value if you don't provide one, so it's still possible to provide values yourself.

ARRAY

The ARRAY data type stores a flat (or one-dimensional) collection of another data type. It's indexable using inverted indexes designed to work with tokenizable data, such as the values of an array or the key-value pairs in a JSON object. Let's create a table with an ARRAY column to learn more about it.

First, we'll create a table with an ARRAY column. Arrays are created in the TYPE[] syntax or the TYPE ARRAY syntax as follows:

```
-- Create with TYPE[] syntax:
CREATE TABLE person (
    id UUID DEFAULT gen_random_uuid() PRIMARY KEY,
    pets STRING[]
);

-- Create with TYPE ARRAY syntax:
CREATE TABLE person (
    id UUID DEFAULT gen_random_uuid() PRIMARY KEY,
    pets STRING ARRAY
);
```

Next, we'll insert some data:

```
INSERT
  INTO person (pets)
VALUES (ARRAY['Max', 'Duke']),
       (ARRAY['Snowball']),
       (ARRAY['Gidgit']),
       (ARRAY['Chloe']);
```

Selecting the values back out of the table reveals their representation in CockroachDB:

```
SELECT * FROM person;
                 id                  |     pets
-------------------------------------+-------------
  59220317-cc79-4689-b05f-c21886a7986d | {Max,Duke}
  5b4455a2-37e7-49de-bd6f-cdd070e8c133 | {Snowball}
  659dce69-03b8-4872-b6af-400e95bf43d9 | {Gidgit}
  f4ef9111-f118-4f66-b950-921d8c1c3291 | {Chloe}
```

There are many operations you can perform against ARRAY columns. We'll cover just the most common.

To return rows that contain a particular value in an ARRAY column, we can use the "contains" operator. The following returns the ID of any person with a pet called Max:

```
SELECT id FROM person WHERE pets @> ARRAY['Max'];
                      id
----------------------------------------
  59220317-cc79-4689-b05f-c21886a7986d
```

To return rows whose ARRAY column is within a given array, we can use the "is contained by" operator. The following returns the ID of any person whose complete list of pets is contained within a given array:

```
SELECT id FROM person WHERE pets <@ ARRAY['Max', 'Duke', 'Snowball'];
                      id
----------------------------------------
  59220317-cc79-4689-b05f-c21886a7986d
  5b4455a2-37e7-49de-bd6f-cdd070e8c133
```

If you know the name of one of a person's pets but not all of them, you can use the overlap operator to find the ID of any person who has a pet contained within a given array:

```
SELECT id FROM person WHERE pets && ARRAY['Max', 'Snowball'];
                      id
----------------------------------------
  59220317-cc79-4689-b05f-c21886a7986d
  5b4455a2-37e7-49de-bd6f-cdd070e8c133
```

Add an element to an array (note that for inserts, you can either use array_append or the append operator ||):

```
UPDATE person
   SET pets = array_append(pets, 'Duke')
 WHERE id = '59220317-cc79-4689-b05f-c21886a7986d';
```

Remove an element from an array:

```
UPDATE person
   SET pets = array_remove(pets, 'Duke')
 WHERE id = '59220317-cc79-4689-b05f-c21886a7986d';
```

To get the most out of an ARRAY column, you'll need to use an inverted index, as without it, CockroachDB will have to perform a full table scan, as highlighted in the following:

```
EXPLAIN SELECT id FROM person WHERE pets @> ARRAY['Max'];
                                        info
---------------------------------------------------------------------------
  distribution: full
  vectorized: true

  • filter
  │ estimated row count: 0
  │ filter: pets @> ARRAY['Max']
  │
  └── • scan
        estimated row count: 4 (100% of the table; stats collected 16
        minutes ago)
        table: person@primary
        spans: FULL SCAN
```

You configure an inverted index on an ARRAY column in a new table as follows:

```
CREATE TABLE person (
    id UUID DEFAULT gen_random_uuid() PRIMARY KEY,
    pets STRING[],
    INVERTED INDEX (pets)
);
```

You configure an inverted index on an ARRAY column in an existing table as follows:

```
CREATE INVERTED INDEX [OPTIONAL_NAME] ON person (pets);
```

BIT

The BIT data type stores a bit array. BIT columns can store varying numbers of bits and can either contain an exact or a variable number of bits:

```
CREATE TABLE bits (
    exactly_1 BIT,
    exactly_64 BIT(64),
```

```
    any_size VARBIT,
    up_to_64 VARBIT(64)
);
```

Values can be inserted into BIT columns as follows (note that the preceding B for each of the values denotes a binary string):

```
INSERT
  INTO bits (exactly_1, exactly_64, any_size, up_to_64)
VALUES (
        B'1',
        B'1010101010101010101010101010101010101010101010101010101
        0101010101010',
        B'10101',
        B'10101010101'
        );
```

BOOL

The BOOL or BOOLEAN data type stores a true or false value and is created as follows:

```
CREATE TABLE person (
      id
            UUID DEFAULT gen_random_uuid() PRIMARY KEY,
      wants_marketing_emails
            BOOL NOT NULL
);
```

Values are provided to BOOL columns with Boolean literals or via type casting from integers:

```
INSERT
  INTO person (wants_marketing_emails)
VALUES
  (1::BOOL),      -- True (any non-zero number)
  (true),         -- Literal true
  (12345::BOOL),  -- True (any non-zero number)
  (0::BOOL),      -- False (zero value)
  (false);        -- Literal false
```

BYTES

The BYTES, BYTEA, or BLOB data type stores the byte array equivalent of TEXT strings and can be created as follows:

```
CREATE TABLE person (
    id
        UUID DEFAULT gen_random_uuid() PRIMARY KEY,
    password
        BYTES NOT NULL
);
```

You can insert BYTES values in several ways. TEXT strings will automatically cast to BYTES, and CockroachDB supports various encoding methods for fine-grained control of insert values:

```
INSERT
  INTO person (password)
VALUES
  ('password'),                      -- String value
  (b'password'),                     -- Byte array literal
  (x'70617373776f7264'),            -- Hex literal
  (b'\x70\x61\x73\x73\x77\x6f\x72\x64'); -- Hex characters
```

Every resulting row from the preceding insert will have an identical password column value.

DATE

The DATE data type stores a day, month, and year value and is created as follows:

```
CREATE TABLE person (
    id
        UUID DEFAULT gen_random_uuid() PRIMARY KEY,
    date_of_birth
        DATE NOT NULL
);
```

Provide values to DATE columns as string literals, interpreted literals, timestamps (which truncate to day precision), or numbers representing the number of *days* since the epoch:

```
INSERT
  INTO person (date_of_birth)
VALUES
  ('1941-09-09'),              -- String literal
  (DATE '1941-09-09'),         -- Interpreted literal
  ('1941-09-09T01:02:03.456Z'), -- Timestamp (will be truncated)
  (CAST(-10341 AS DATE));      -- Number of days since the epoch
```

Every resulting row from the preceding insert will have an identical date_of_birth column value.

ENUM

The ENUM data type provides an enumeration that is validated upon insert and is created as follows:

```
CREATE TYPE planet AS ENUM (
      'mercury',
      'venus',
      'earth',
      'mars',
      'jupiter',
      'saturn',
      'uranus',
      'neptune'
);

CREATE TABLE person (
      id
            UUID DEFAULT gen_random_uuid() PRIMARY KEY,
      favourite_planet
            planet NOT NULL
);
```

As with many of CockroachDB's data types, ENUM columns are castable from string literals, interpreted literals, or strings with direct casts:

```
INSERT
  INTO person (favourite_planet)
VALUES
  ('neptune'),                -- String literal
  (planet 'earth'),           -- Interpreted literal
  (CAST('saturn' AS planet)); -- Cast
```

DECIMAL

The DECIMAL, DEC, or NUMERIC data type stores exact, fixed-point[2] numbers of variable size and is created either with or without a precision.

Let's start by creating a DECIMAL column without specifying a precision and scale:

```
CREATE TABLE person (
     id
           UUID DEFAULT gen_random_uuid() PRIMARY KEY,
     bitcoin_balance
           DECIMAL NOT NULL
);
```

Inserting some values into this table will reveal that only the digits required to represent the number are used:

```
INSERT
  INTO person (bitcoin_balance)
VALUES
  (0.000030),
  (0.80),
  (147.50);
```

---

[2] Meaning the number of digits after the decimal point is fixed.

```
SELECT * FROM person;
                    id                  | bitcoin_balance
----------------------------------------+------------------
  2880768d-802f-4096-933d-68be971b3a73 |          147.50
  975d5aa2-7769-48e1-99dc-693b6a3fc07f |            0.80
  f8a19a8f-c40c-4b6d-b186-18688f020f2b |        0.000030
```

Now, let's recreate the table and provide a precision and scale for the DECIMAL column this time. The DECIMAL column type now takes two arguments: the first defines the precision of the value, and the second defines the scale. The precision argument tells CockroachDB the maximum number of integral digits (digits to the left of the decimal point) and fractional digits (digitals to the right of the decimal point):

```
CREATE TABLE person (
    id
        UUID DEFAULT gen_random_uuid() PRIMARY KEY,
    bitcoin_balance
        DECIMAL(16, 8) NOT NULL
);
```

Inserting some values into this table will reveal that all eight of the fractional digits are used:

```
INSERT
  INTO person (bitcoin_balance)
VALUES
  (0.000030),
  (0.80),
  (147.50);

SELECT * FROM person;
                    id                  | bitcoin_balance
----------------------------------------+------------------
  8de29c92-13f8-4f4c-abef-62c7ff3cdb87 |      0.00003000
  ee2e01fa-7ff0-4a10-9c09-f2e607e6ec49 |      0.80000000
  f9180229-d42f-45b5-b6fc-914396219da8 |    147.50000000
```

It is possible to insert infinite and NAN (not a number) values in a `DECIMAL` column as follows:

```
INSERT
  INTO person (bitcoin_balance)
VALUES
  ('inf'), ('infinity'), ('+inf'), ('+infinity'),
  ('-inf'), ('-infinity'),
  ('nan');
```

Positive infinity Bitcoin. One can dream.

FLOAT

The `FLOAT`, `FLOAT4` (`REAL`), and `FLOAT8` (`DOUBLE PRECISION`) data types store inexact, floating-point numbers with up to 17 digits of precision and are created as follows:

```
CREATE TABLE person (
    id
        UUID DEFAULT gen_random_uuid() PRIMARY KEY,
    latitude
        FLOAT NOT NULL,
    longitude
        FLOAT NOT NULL
);
```

```
INSERT
  INTO person (latitude, longitude)
VALUES
  (38.908200917747095, -77.03236828895616),
  (52.382578005867906, 4.855332269875395),
  (51.46112343492288, -0.11128454244911225),
  (51.514018690098645, -0.1267503331073194);
```

```
SELECT * FROM person;
                     id          | latitude           | longitude
----------------------------------+--------------------+----------
  19f0cfcc-a073-4d96-850c-e121f1e940b6 | 52.382578005867906 |
4.855332269875395
  78a03a7c-afe4-4196-bc0c-0e86841373e4 | 51.46112343492288  |
-0.11128454244911225
  9c68004e-2265-4ebf-b14c-20fa6292dc6c | 38.908200917747095 |
-77.03236828895616
  a9b502c0-8ffd-4e75-a796-4e87554a3ebd | 51.514018690098645 |
-0.1267503331073194
```

INET

The INET data type stores valid IPv4 and IPv6 addresses and CIDRs (Classless Inter-Domain Routing) and is created as follows:

```
CREATE TABLE person (
    id
        UUID DEFAULT gen_random_uuid() PRIMARY KEY,
    ip
        INET NOT NULL
);
```

Inserting some values into this table will reveal that CockroachDB understands the IP addresses being inserted and removes any redundant masks:

```
INSERT
  INTO person (ip)
VALUES
  ('10.0.1.0/24'),
  ('10.0.1.1/32'),
  ('229a:d983:f190:75ef:5f06:a5a8:f5c2:8500/128'),
  ('229a:d983:f190:75ef:5f06:a5a8:f5c2:853f/100');
```

```
SELECT * FROM person;
                    id                 |                  ip
---------------------------------------+--------------------------------
  29121f2e-e977-474b-9fb5-818399ed7b9f | 10.0.1.0/24
  5cce3936-9f27-4e00-b0dc-9866e621270f | 10.0.1.1
  9b53053d-ce6e-416a-9b63-9d0bc9bc9870 | 229a:d983:f190:75ef:5f06:a5a8:
                                         f5c2:8500
  d383ef34-b24d-48b8-b008-57f4e001faa3 | 229a:d983:f190:75ef:5f06:a5a8:
                                         f5c2:853f/100
```

Notice that the 10.0.1.0/24 address keeps its mask because a /24 mask for this address includes addresses from 10.0.1.0 to 10.0.1.255. On the other hand, the 10.0.1.1/32 address has a mask of /32, which means "this IP address only," meaning we have a specific IP address, and the mask is superfluous. The same holds for the IPv6 addresses, where a /128 means "this IP address only."

INTERVAL

The INTERVAL data type stores durations ranging from microseconds to years and is created as follows:

```
CREATE TABLE rodeo_records (
    id
        UUID DEFAULT gen_random_uuid() PRIMARY KEY,
    duration
        INTERVAL NOT NULL
);
```

You can provide durations as ISO 8601 strings, time strings, and seconds. Selecting the rows out of the table reveals how the values are stored and how you can cast them to seconds:

```
INSERT
    INTO rodeo_records (duration)
VALUES
    ('10:45:00.0'), -- Time string
    ('1h30m'),      -- ISO 8601 string
    (30::INTERVAL); -- Seconds
```

```
SELECT id, duration, duration::INT FROM rodeo_records;
                    id                  | duration | duration
----------------------------------------+----------+----------
  102cbbc8-6001-4642-b7e4-b4cbd9b03d35  | 10:45:00 |    38700
  665f4306-0407-4d48-ab1c-4c628cd3e1d3  | 01:30:00 |     5400
  7fbf8859-65fa-4100-ae61-f9bff76b89ec  | 00:00:30 |       30
```

JSONB

The JSONB, JSON data type stores arbitrary JSON objects and is ideal for storing semi-structured data (data that has a structure that doesn't fit or may outgrow your relational database tables). JSONB columns can be created as follows:

```
CREATE TABLE song (
    id
        UUID DEFAULT gen_random_uuid() PRIMARY KEY,
    details
        JSONB NOT NULL
);
```

If you plan on performing complex queries against a JSON column, you'll want to create an inverted index for the column. I'll cover these in a subsequent chapter on performance.

To insert data into a JSONB column, simply provide a JSON string as follows:

```
INSERT
    INTO song (details)
VALUES
    ('{"label": "Century Media", "release_date": "2004-09-20"}'),
    ('{"label": "Season of Mist", "release_date": "2010-02-15"}'),
    ('{"label": "Season of Mist", "release_date": "2016-02-12"}');
```

JSON columns are very flexible. You can query their fields and select specific values to return. Let's do both now. The following query returns the release dates of songs released under the "Season of Mist" record label as string values:

```
SELECT
    details->>'release_date' AS release_date
FROM
    song
WHERE
    details @> '{"label": "Season of Mist"}';

  release_date
---------------
  2010-02-15
  2016-02-12
```

To access specific JSON fields as regular columns, create indexes or even create PRIMARY KEYs from JSON fields within JSON documents; this is also possible with the JSON data type.

The following CREATE statement recreates the table, but this time, its id and label columns are from fields in the details JSON column:

```
CREATE TABLE song (
    id
        UUID PRIMARY KEY AS ((details->>'id')::UUID) STORED,
    label
        TEXT AS ((details->>'label')::TEXT) STORED,
    details
        JSONB NOT NULL,
    INDEX (label),
    INVERTED INDEX idx_details(details)
);

INSERT
    INTO song (details)
VALUES
    ('{"id":"60d28ed4-ee97-43d5-98a7-ba42d478f4c7", "label": "Century
    Media", "release_date": "2004-09-20"}'),
    ('{"id":"4b158ac6-386d-4143-8281-ca6f0f9c9a93", "label": "Season of
    Mist", "release_date": "2010-02-15"}'),
    ('{"id":"c82dc39d-f310-45a4-9a31-805d923f1c8e", "label": "Season of
    Mist", "release_date": "2016-02-12"}');
```

We can now treat the *id* and *label* columns exactly as we'd treat any other database column:

```
SELECT
      id,
      label,
      details->>'release_date' release_date
FROM
      song
WHERE
      label = 'Season of Mist';
```

SERIAL

The SERIAL data type is not strictly a data type but rather an INT, INT2, INT4, or INT8 with a default value applied, resulting in an auto-incrementing number. SERIAL was introduced to CockroachDB to provide Postgres compatibility. As such, you should consider using the UUID data type with a default value of gen_random_uuid() instead of the SERIAL data type, as this provides 128 bits of randomness vs. SERIAL's maximum of 64 bits.

SERIAL columns can be created as follows:

```
CREATE TABLE random (
      r1
            SERIAL2, -- 16-bits AKA SMALLSERIAL
      r2
            SERIAL4, -- 32-bits
      r3
            SERIAL8  -- 64-bits AKA SERIAL or BIGSERIAL
);
```

Inserting data into this table will reveal that close attention to the SERIAL documentation[3] is required to fully understand the nuances of this data type:

---

[3] www.cockroachlabs.com/docs/stable/serial.html

```
INSERT
  INTO random
DEFAULT VALUES;

SELECT * FROM random;
          r1             |         r2           |          r3
--------------------+--------------------+--------------------
  698584214451748865 | 698584214451781633 | 698584214451814401
  698584216070979585 | 698584216071012353 | 698584216071045121
  698584216921047041 | 698584216921079809 | 698584216921112577
  698584217849954305 | 698584217849987073 | 698584217850019841
```

As we can see from the values generated, regardless of the integer size provided by the data type definition, the default mode for generating these values (unique_rowid()) will always result in a 64-bit integer.

STRING

The STRING, TEXT, CHARACTER, CHAR, or VARCHAR data type stores either fixed or variable-length strings of Unicode characters and is created as follows:

```
CREATE TABLE person (
    id
        UUID DEFAULT gen_random_uuid() PRIMARY KEY,
    first_name
        TEXT NOT NULL,
    last_name
        VARCHAR(50) NOT NULL,
    grade
        CHAR NOT NULL
);
```

By showing the columns of our table, we can see what the data types resolve to behind the scenes:

```
SELECT column_name, data_type
FROM [SHOW columns FROM person];
```

```
column_name |  data_type
--------------+--------------
 id           | UUID
 first_name   | STRING
 last_name    | VARCHAR(50)
 grade        | CHAR
```

Note that VARCHAR(n) is, in fact, an alias of STRING(n), but for Postgres compatibility, it is still represented as VARCHAR(n) here, as Postgres does not have a STRING data type.

Inserting data into this table will reveal that CockroachDB faithfully represents Unicode characters:

```
INSERT
  INTO person (first_name, last_name, grade)
VALUES
     ('ゆきひろ', 'まつもと', 'A'),
     ('Rob', 'Reid', 'B'),
     ('☺', '☹', 'C');

SELECT * FROM person;
                 id                 | first_name | last_name | grade
------------------------------------+------------+-----------+--------
  6bb12902-ef0d-4586-afea-8ac003ce284a | Rob        | Reid      | B
  6d720a57-6067-4b95-b9a5-7dfc8ef192e0 | ゆきひろ    | まつもと   | A
  75098f20-1c38-49ec-91fb-60acfc8d6463 | ☺          | ☹         | C
```

As in Postgres, you'll receive an error from CockroachDB if you try to insert data that will not fit into a fixed-length or limited variable-length column.

TIME/TIMETZ

The TIME and TIMEZ data types store time (minus date) values in UTC and zoned representations, respectively. They can store time values to various levels of precision, ranging from second precision down to microsecond precision.

Cockroach Labs recommends using the TIME variant and converting to local time in the front-end.

```
CREATE TABLE schedule (
      name STRING(50)
NOT NULL,
      time_of_day TIME NOT NULL
);
INSERT INTO schedule (name, time_of_day)
VALUES
      ('Take dogs for walk', '10:30:00'),
      ('Make lunch', '12:00:00');
SELECT * FROM schedule;
```

```
          name         | time_of_day
---------------------+--------------

  Take dogs for walk | 10:30:00

  Make lunch         | 12:00:00
```

TIMESTAMP/TIMESTAMPTZ

The TIMESTAMP and TIMESTAMPTZ data types store timestamps in UTC and *display* the values in UTC and zoned representations, respectively.

Cockroach Labs recommends using the TIMESTAMPTZ data type over the TIMESTAMP data type for explicitness, so I'll demonstrate the use of the TIMESTAMPTZ data type, which is created as follows:

```
CREATE TABLE episode_schedule (
    id
        UUID DEFAULT gen_random_uuid() PRIMARY KEY,
    name
        TEXT NOT NULL,
    next_show_time
        TIMESTAMPTZ(0) NOT NULL
);
```

As you can see, the TIMESTAMP data types allow for an optional precision to be provided. This precision accepts a value between zero (representing second precision) and six (representing microsecond precision). The default precision for TIMESTAMP data types is 6, so for most cases, you can omit the precision entirely.

Let's insert some data into the table to show its representation to users in different time zones:

```
INSERT
  INTO episode_schedule (name, next_show_time)
VALUES
      ('South Park - The Tail of Sc...', '2021-12-10 22:00:00+00:00'),
      ('South Park - Grounded Vinda...', '2021-12-10 22:30:00+00:00'),
      ('South Park - Make Love, Not...', '2021-12-10 23:00:00+00:00');
```

Let's select the rows out of the table now, once for users in a UTC time zone and once for users in the Eastern Daylight Time (EDT) time zone:

```
SET TIME ZONE 'UTC';
SELECT next_show_time FROM episode_schedule;
      next_show_time
-------------------------
  2021-12-10 23:00:00+00
  2021-12-10 22:30:00+00
  2021-12-10 22:00:00+00

SET TIME ZONE 'America/New_York';
SELECT next_show_time FROM episode_schedule;
      next_show_time
-------------------------
  2021-12-10 18:00:00-05
  2021-12-10 17:30:00-05
  2021-12-10 17:00:00-05
```

As you can see, users in the UTC time zone see the data as it was inserted into the database, while users in the EDT time zone see the data in their local time as a -05:00 offset from UTC.

GEOMETRY

The GEOMETRY and GEOGRAPHY data types store spatial objects on variable-plane[4] geometry and earth positions as spheroids, respectively, and are created as follows:

```
CREATE TABLE property (
    id
        UUID DEFAULT gen_random_uuid() PRIMARY KEY,
    location
        GEOMETRY NOT NULL,
    INVERTED INDEX (location)
);
```

Both the GEOMETRY and GEOGRAPHY data types can store the following spatial objects:

- GEOMETRYCOLLECTION – A collection of other spatial objects (including other GEOMETRYCOLLECTION objects)

- LINESTRING – A collection of points making up an arbitrary line, useful for roads and rivers

- MULTILINESTRING – A collection of LINESTRING objects

- MULTIPOINT – A collection of POINT objects

- MULTIPOLYGON – A collection of POLYGON objects

- POINT – Two points that represent coordinates (e.g., latitude and longitude)

- POLYGON – A collection of points that represent an area

Let's insert some GEOMETRY data into our table and perform some basic operations on it. In this scenario, let's assume we provide a service that allows users to look up stores. We hold the store locations, and users draw search areas to find them.

```
INSERT
    INTO property (location)
VALUES
    ('POINT(-0.16197244907496533 51.50186005364136)'),
```

---

[4] 2D, 3D, etc.

```
('POINT(-0.16139087662866003 51.498542352748814)'),
('POINT(-0.17528813494181622 51.48604279157454)');
```

A particularly wealthy user wishes to search for property in the Knightsbridge area of London and provides the following coordinates:

```
SELECT id FROM property
WHERE ST_CoveredBy(
    location,
    'POLYGON((-0.1642155647277832 51.496975050193456,
-0.15342235565185544 51.496975050193456, -0.15342235565185544
51.50344015477113, -0.1642155647277832 51.50344015477113,
-0.1642155647277832 51.496975050193456))'
);
                    id
----------------------------------------
  7a37b426-c87e-454e-9d67-2848e05f8326
  de7425c9-9939-4e3c-9f48-f9fabdfca9df
```

Their query returns just the two properties in Knightsbridge, leaving the equally lavish Chelsea property for another fabulously wealthy user.

A very neat feature of Postgres and CockroachDB is the ability to convert GEOMETRY data into GeoJSON; let's convert the search area provided by the user into GeoJSON and visualize it on https://geojson.io:

```
SELECT ST_AsGeoJSON('POLYGON((-0.1642155647277832 51.496975050193456,
-0.15342235565185544 51.496975050193456, -0.15342235565185544
51.50344015477113, -0.1642155647277832 51.50344015477113,
-0.1642155647277832 51.496975050193456))');
```

```
{"type":"Polygon","coordinates":[[[-0.164215565,51.49697505],
[-0.153422356,51.49697505],[-0.153422356,51.503440155],
[-0.164215565,51.503440155],[-0.164215565,51.49697505]]]}
```

Pasting this data into the GeoJSON website yields the user's search area as shown in Figure 3-2.

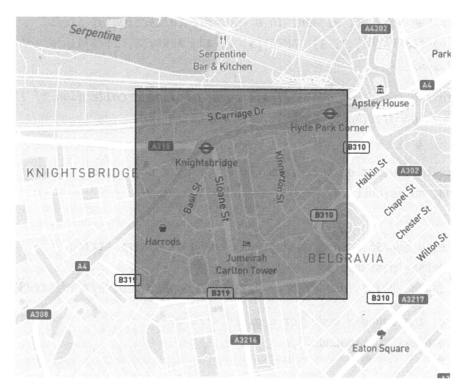

Figure 3-2. *A GeoJSON polygon on* `https://geojson.io`

Functions

CockroachDB provides built-in functions to make certain operations easier, and there are functions for working with most of the data types introduced in this chapter.

Built-in functions[5] either provide functionality for working with data types or expose core system functionality such as working with stream ingestion and getting system information.

I will demonstrate the use of a small selection of built-in functions, but for brevity, I will leave the exploration of the remaining functions as an exercise to the reader. The following code example shows some of the more commonly used functions, and the comment preceding each provides a brief explanation.

```
-- Return the largest element in a variadic collection of items.
SELECT greatest(ARRAY[1, 2, 3], ARRAY[1, 2, 4], ARRAY[1, 2, 2]);
--> {1,2,4}
```

---

[5]`www.cockroachlabs.com/docs/stable/functions-and-operators.html#built-in-functions`

```
-- Return the smallest element in a variadic collection of items.
SELECT least(ARRAY[1, 2, 3], ARRAY[1, 2, 4], ARRAY[1, 2, 2]);
--> {1,2,2}

-- Return the number of non-null items in a variadic collection of items.
SELECT num_nonnulls(NULL, 1, NULL, 'a', NULL);
--> 2

-- Return the number of null items in a variadic collection of items.
SELECT num_nulls(NULL, 1, NULL, 'a', NULL);
--> 3

-- Creates a SHA256 hash from a given string or binary string.
SELECT sha256('password');
--> 5e884898da28047151d0e56f8dc6292773603d0d6aabbdd62a11ef721d1542d8

-- Returns the Soundex code for a given string.
SELECT soundex('cockroachdb');
--> C262

-- Returns the start position of a substring.
SELECT strpos('cockroachdb', 'db');
--> 10

-- Encodes a value into its hexadecimal representation.
SELECT to_hex('cockroachdb');
--> 636f636b726f6163686462

-- Decodes a value from its encoded representation (out of hex, escape, and
base64).
SELECT decode('636f636b726f6163686462', 'hex');
--> cockroachdb

-- Converts an X, Y coordinate (or longitude, latitude) to a POINT
geometry.
SELECT st_point(-0.667790874, 51.922472692);
--> 0101000000054B68CF78A5EE5BFEACBCD9513F64940
```

```
-- Converts a GEOMETRY type to its GeoJSON representation.
SELECT st_asgeojson('010100000054B68CF78A5EE5BFEACBCD9513F64940');
--> {"type":"Point","coordinates":[-0.667790874,51.922472692]}

-- Returns the host bitmask from a CIDR.
SELECT hostmask('10.1.0.0/16');
--> 0.0.255.255

-- Returns the network bits mask used from a CIDR.
SELECT netmask('10.1.0.0/16');
--> 255.255.0.0

-- Gets a value out of a JSON object using dot-notation.
SELECT json_extract_path('{"first_name": "rob", "last_name": "reid"}',
'first_name');
--> "rob"

-- Sets a value in a JSON object using dot-notation.
SELECT json_set('{"first_name": "Rob", "last_name": "Reid"}', array['first_
name'], '"Emily"');
--> {"first_name": "Emily", "last_name": "Reid"}

-- Determines whether a value exists in a JSON object using dot-notation.
SELECT jsonb_exists_any('{"foo": "bar"}', array['foo']);
--> true

-- Truncates a date beyond a given precision.
SELECT date_trunc('hour', '2021-10-07 18:26:37.241363+00'::TIMESTAMP);
--> 2021-10-07 18:00:00

-- Returns the difference between two dates.
SELECT age(now(), '1941-09-09');
--> 80 years 28 days 18:30:15.845593
```

There are many more functions to try; for a complete list of available functions, visit
www.cockroachlabs.com/docs/stable/functions-and-operators.html.

Geo-partitioned Data

Geo-partitioning is one of CockroachDB's most powerful Enterprise features, and as of v21.1.10, working with geo-partitioned data has become much more straightforward.

To get started with geo-partitioned data, you first need to decide on a partitioning strategy. For example, will all of the rows within a table need to remain in one location, or will specific rows within that table need to be separated by location? If you need all of the rows within a table to remain in one location, the REGION BY TABLE table locality is what you need. On the other hand, if you need to pin rows to different places, the REGION BY ROW table locality is a good choice.

Let's create some database tables to demonstrate geo-partitioning for both locality strategies.

Before we start, let's create a cluster that spans multiple continents. Start by creating a temporary Enterprise cluster using CockroachDB's demo command:

```
$ cockroach demo \
--no-example-database \
--nodes 9 \
--insecure \
--demo-locality=region=us-east1,az=a:region=us-east1,az=b:region=us-
east1,az=c:region=asia-northeast1,az=a:region=asia-
northeast1,az=b:region=asia-northeast1,az=c:region=europe-
west1,az=a:region=europe-west1,az=b:region=europe-west1,az=c
```

This command creates an insecure, empty cluster with nine nodes. The --demo-locality argument allows us to specify the region and availability zones for the nodes to be distributed across: nine availability zones, one for each of our nine nodes. The syntax of this argument's value looks tricky but is actually very simple; for each of the requested localities, we simply provide a colon-separated collection of region and availability zone pairs.

In order for CockroachDB to show a map of your cluster in its Node Map view, we need to run a SQL command in the CockroachDB shell. At the time of writing, only a handful of locations are configured in the system.locations table; both the United States and Europe are configured, but Asia is not. We need to tell CockroachDB where to place the asia-northeast1 cluster on its Node Map, and the following statement does just that:

```
INSERT into system.locations VALUES ('region', 'asia-northeast1',
35.689487, 139.691706);
```

Open a browser to `http://localhost:8080/#/overview/map` and you'll see a visual representation of your new cluster such as that shown in Figure 3-3.

Figure 3-3. *The CockroachDB Node Map view of our cluster*

It's now time to create some partitioned tables.

Whether we're pinning table or row data, we need to make CockroachDB region-aware. The following statements create three regions in the database. These match the three regions we created when initializing the cluster with the demo command.

```
ALTER DATABASE defaultdb PRIMARY REGION "europe-west1";
ALTER DATABASE defaultdb ADD REGION "us-east1";
ALTER DATABASE defaultdb ADD REGION "asia-northeast1";
```

As discussed in Chapter 2, it's vital you correctly set regional or zonal survival goals for your databases. While it is not essential to geo-partitioning, it is helpful to know how your database will function in the event of an outage.

```
ALTER DATABASE defaultdb SURVIVE REGION FAILURE;
```

REGION BY ROW

The REGION BY ROW table locality ensures that individual rows within a table are pinned to specific locations, depending on values set for a specific field. In human speak, a location can be a continent, a country, a state, or even a specific machine. In infrastructure speak, a location can be a region, an availability zone, or a node.

First, we'll create a database for this example and make it region-aware. The following code statements create a database and attach regions and a primary region via ALTER statements:

```
CREATE DATABASE my_app;

USE my_app;

ALTER DATABASE my_app PRIMARY REGION "europe-west1";
ALTER DATABASE my_app ADD REGION "us-east1";
ALTER DATABASE my_app ADD REGION "asia-northeast1";
```

We don't need to manually set a survival goal in this example because for now, we'll stick with the default configuration, which allows CockroachDB to survive zonal failures.

Next, we'll create a table. This table will have two columns that allow us to geo-partition data:

- **country** – The country that is associated with the row.

- **crdb_region** – The region that describes where CockroachDB will pin data. This column is populated automatically on-insert with a value derived from the country column. Using a case statement, we'll ensure that when the country column is "JP" for Japan, "KR" for South Korea, or "TH" for Thailand, the crdb_region column receives the value "asia-northwest1", etc.

The following code creates a table called "person" with the aforementioned geo-partitioning columns. It ensures that locality rules for the table are set to REGIONAL BY ROW, meaning each row will be pinned to a different region:

```
CREATE TABLE person (
    id
        UUID DEFAULT gen_random_uuid() PRIMARY KEY,
    country
        TEXT NOT NULL,
    crdb_region crdb_internal_region NOT NULL AS (
      CASE
          WHEN country IN ('JP', 'KR', 'TH') THEN 'asia-northeast1'
          WHEN country IN ('DE', 'FR', 'UK') THEN 'europe-west1'
```

```
        WHEN country IN ('BR', 'MX', 'US') THEN 'us-east1'
        ELSE 'europe-west1'
    END
  ) STORED
);
```

```
ALTER TABLE "person" SET LOCALITY REGIONAL BY ROW;
```

Next, we'll insert some data into the person table. We'll provide different country codes to ensure that data is stored across each of our three regions.

```
INSERT into person (country)
VALUES
    ('JP'), ('KR'), -- Japan and South Korea -> asia-northeast1
    ('DE'), ('FR'), -- German and France -> europe-west1
    ('BR'), ('MX'); -- Brazil and Mexico -> us-east1
```

Selecting the values back out of the person table reveals that the crdb_region column is populated as expected:

```
SELECT * FROM person;
                  id                | country |   crdb_region
------------------------------------+---------+------------------
  3a77bfcf-e289-4e47-8e11-7ca0b77ade72 | FR    | europe-west1
  bc5f5bef-72b4-4c7a-a7d8-0ece1345a7e1 | DE    | europe-west1
  74a1c95b-c5a4-46ae-bd8d-d049514fb728 | BR    | us-east1
  477cbdc6-fe0f-436c-99fd-0f28866d394a | KR    | asia-northeast1
  8c5e8b31-c361-4157-8671-b723cfcf0e06 | MX    | us-east1
  e8a6760f-9596-4b4c-838b-94eb2098a73e | JP    | asia-northeast1
```

By default, CockroachDB will use a replication factor of five for the person table. You can confirm this with a query for the table's RANGES (I've modified the formatting to make it easier to read):

```
SELECT lease_holder_locality, replicas, replica_localities
FROM [SHOW RANGES FROM TABLE person]
WHERE start_key NOT LIKE '%Prefix%';
```

```
region=asia-northeast1,az=c
{3,4,5,6,7} {"region=us-east1,az=c","region=asia-
northeast1,az=a","region=asia-northeast1,az=b","region=asia-
northeast1,az=c","region=europe-west1,az=a"}

region=europe-west1,az=a
{3,6,7,8,9}
{"region=us-east1,az=c","region=asia-northeast1,az=c","region=europe-
west1,az=a","region=europe-west1,az=b","region=europe-west1,az=c"}

region=us-east1,az=b
{1,2,3,5,7}
{"region=us-east1,az=a","region=us-east1,az=b","region=us-
east1,az=c","region=asia-northeast1,az=b","region=europe-west1,az=a"}
```

From the preceding output, you'll see that data in the person table is shared across five nodes, as per the default replication factor in CockroachDB. A replication factor of five provides additional robustness if a region becomes unavailable.

I'll now drop the replication factor from five to three to show how CockroachDB will keep geo-partitioned data pinned to the regions specified in crdb_internal_region columns (in our case, the crdb_region column):

```
SET override_multi_region_zone_config = true;

ALTER TABLE person CONFIGURE ZONE USING num_replicas = 3;
```

The preceding ALTER statement will be blocked by CockroachDB, as any request to update the number of replicas in a table or database requires special permissions. However, as seen in the preceding statement, we can ask CockroachDB to permit us to make this change by overriding the multiregion zone configuration flag.

Over the next ~30 seconds, you'll see CockroachDB reduce the number of replicas for the person table from five to three. Replicas are now pinned to the respective regions.

```
SELECT lease_holder_locality, replicas, replica_localities
FROM [SHOW RANGES FROM TABLE person]
WHERE start_key NOT LIKE '%Prefix%';

region=asia-northeast1,az=c
{4,5,6}
```

```
{"region=asia-northeast1,az=a","region=asia-northeast1,az=b",
"region=asia-northeast1,az=c"}

region=europe-west1,az=a
{7,8,9}
{"region=europe-west1,az=a","region=europe-west1,az=b",
"region=europe-west1,az=c"}

region=us-east1,az=b
{1,2,3}
{"region=us-east1,az=a","region=us-east1,az=b","region=us-east1,az=c"}
```

REGION BY TABLE

The REGION BY TABLE table locality ensures that all of the rows within a table remain in a particular location. In human speak, a location can be a continent, a country, a state, or even a specific machine. In infrastructure speak, a location can be a region, an availability zone, or a node.

The REGION BY TABLE table locality is the default configuration for tables in CockroachDB. As a result, access to regional tables will be faster when accessed from the database's primary region.

Use this option if you wish to pin all data within a table to one region. In the following example, we'll create a regional table.

First, we'll create a table. Note that in this example, I'm not providing any regional information to the rows of the table; this is because the table itself is regional.

```
CREATE TABLE american_scientists (
    id
        UUID DEFAULT gen_random_uuid() PRIMARY KEY,
    first_name
        TEXT NOT NULL,
    last_name
        TEXT NOT NULL
);

INSERT into american_scientists (first_name, last_name)
VALUES
```

```
('Grace', 'Hopper'),
('Barbara', 'McClintock'),
('Rachel', 'Carson');
```

Assuming the database's primary region is still set to europe-west1 from the REGION BY ROW example, if we were to select the table's ranges at this point, we'd see that a European-based leaseholder currently manages our American scientists:

```
SELECT lease_holder_locality, replicas, replica_localities
FROM [SHOW RANGES FROM TABLE american_scientists];
```

```
region=europe-west1,az=a
{3,4,7,8,9}
{"region=us-east1,az=c","region=asia-northeast1,az=a","region=europe-
west1,az=a","region=europe-west1,az=b","region=europe-west1,az=c"}
```

To move this table into the us-east1 region, we need to run a couple of simple statements. First, set the database's primary region to us-east1, which will update the leaseholder for the data but will not physically locate all replicas to the United States. CockroachDB sets a default number of replicas for a new table to five, so as we have only three nodes in the us-east1 region, CockroachDB will use nodes from other regions to bring the replica count up to five:

```
ALTER DATABASE my_app PRIMARY REGION "us-east1";
```

```
SELECT lease_holder_locality, replicas, replica_localities
FROM [SHOW RANGES FROM TABLE american_scientists];
```

```
region=us-east1,az=c
{1,2,3,4,8}
{"region=us-east1,az=a","region=us-east1,az=b","region=us-
east1,az=c","region=asia-northeast1,az=a","region=europe-west1,az=b"}
```

Next, drop the replica count down to three to ensure that all data moves across to the three nodes in the us-east1 region:

```
SET override_multi_region_zone_config = true;
```

```
ALTER TABLE american_scientists CONFIGURE ZONE USING num_replicas = 3;
```

```
SELECT lease_holder_locality, replicas, replica_localities
FROM [SHOW RANGES FROM TABLE american_scientists];

region=us-east1,az=c
{1,2,3}
{"region=us-east1,az=a","region=us-east1,az=b","region=us-east1,az=c"}
```

In the previous step, we reduced the number of replicas for the american_scientists table from five to three. Doing so will impact the resilience of the cluster, given that CockroachDB will now replicate data across fewer nodes. In later chapters, I share some cluster size and replication number recommendations for production environments.

CHAPTER 4

Managing CockroachDB from the Command Line

As we discovered in Chapter 2, CockroachDB can be installed in many ways. A great way to create databases during development is to use the cockroach binary. In this chapter, we'll explore the cockroach binary and the features it provides.

The Cockroach Binary

The cockroach binary uses the https://github.com/spf13/cobra library to manage commands and subcommands. Cobra is a popular Go package for creating rich CLIs (Command-Line Interfaces) used by many popular CLIs, including docker and kubectl. It will be familiar to users of either.

Commands in the cockroach binary are hierarchical and start with the cockroach "root" command itself. A set of subcommands are exposed in a tree-like structure, as shown in Figure 4-1.

© Rob Reid 2022
R. Reid, *Practical CockroachDB*, https://doi.org/10.1007/978-1-4842-8224-3_4

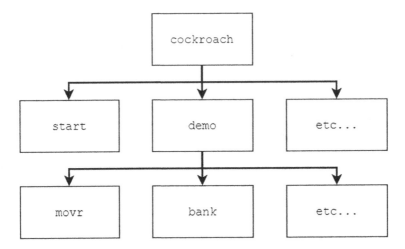

Figure 4-1. *A tree that represents the commands under the* cockroach *binary*

Navigate the command tree by entering a subcommand and using the --help argument at each level. For example:

```
$ cockroach -h
$ cockroach start -h
$ cockroach demo bank
```

The start and start-single-node Commands

CockroachDB provides separate commands for starting single-node and multinode clusters. Use start-single-node to create a single-node cluster and start to create a multinode cluster.

At first, it might seem clunky to have two commands to start clusters. Shouldn't it be possible to use the start command for both? The requirements of a single-node vs. multinode cluster are different, so having two commands prevents you from creating inappropriately sized clusters.

We've created multiple clusters in the previous chapters, so I won't labor the start and start-single-node commands here. I will, however, demonstrate the differences and why it's necessary to get them right.

Starting a multinode cluster using the cockroach binary is a two-step process involving the start and init commands. First, you run the start command to create the nodes and configure them.

The start command requires a --join argument that takes the addresses of other nodes in the cluster, forcing you to think about the basic topology of your cluster and how the nodes will find one another. Cockroach Labs recommends configuring between three and five nodes in the --join argument to ensure the startup performance of your node.

After starting your nodes, you run the init command to initialize the cluster nodes. In a nutshell, the init command initializes the database engine on each node and ensures they are running the same version of CockroachDB.

To start a single-node CockroachDB cluster, use the start-single-node command. This command starts a node and initializes it, meaning you don't have to run the init command as you would with a multinode cluster.

Unlike the start command, the start-single-node command does not allow you to pass a --join argument, forcing your cluster to remain as a single node.

The demo Command

As discussed in Chapter 2, the demo command starts an in-memory Enterprise cluster, allowing you to try out all of the features of CockroachDB Enterprise on your local machine.

The demo command allows you to create an empty database and comes with a handful of preloaded sample databases to give you a head start. A call to the cockroach demo command with the -h or --help argument will list these databases:

```
$ cockroach demo --help
```

The list of sample databases currently includes the following databases:

- **bank** – A sample database with a single table containing accounts and balances

- **intro** – A sample database with a single table containing the ASCII representation of a cockroach stored across multiple lines in a table

- **kv** – A sample database with a single key-value table

- **movr** – A sample database that represents the data store for a fictional ride-sharing application

- **startrek** – A sample database with two related tables: one that stores Star Trek episodes and one that stores the quotes from them

- **tpcc** – A sample database representing the data store for a fictional commerce business that's ready to be hit by TPC-C[1] benchmarks

- **ycsb** – A sample database with a single table containing user data, ready to be hit by the Yahoo! Cloud Serving Benchmark[2]

For most use cases, you'll want to start an empty database. I do just this in Chapter 3 as follows:

```
$ cockroach demo \
--no-example-database \
--nodes 9 \
--demo-locality=region=us-east1,az=a:region=us-east1,az=b:region=us-
east1,az=c:region=asia-northeast1,az=a:region=asia-
northeast1,az=b:region=asia-northeast1,az=c:region=europe-
west1,az=a:region=europe-west1,az=b:region=europe-west1,az=c
```

The cert Command

The cockroach cert command initializes all of the certificates you'll need to run and connect to a CockroachDB cluster. There are four main subcommands to be aware of:

- **create-ca** – Create a Certificate Authority (CA) certificate that you can use to create node and client certificates.

- **create-node** – Create a certificate and key to use for cluster nodes.

- **create-client** – Create a certificate and key to use for client connections.

- **list** – List the certificates in a given certificate directory (--cert-dir) or ${HOME}/.cockroach-certs if empty.

---

[1]www.tpc.org/tpcc
[2]https://github.com/brianfrankcooper/YCSB

We'll explore the create-* subcommands of the cockroach cert command in Chapter 6 to create a secure cluster. Let's see what the list subcommand does here:

```
$ cockroach cert list --certs-dir certs
Certificate directory: certs
  Usage  | Certificate File |    Key File     |  Expires   |         Notes         |
---------+------------------+-----------------+------------+-----------------------+
  CA     | ca.crt           |                 | 2031/10/28 | num certs: 1          |
  Node   | node.crt         | node.key        | 2026/10/24 | addresses: localhost  |
  Client | client.root.crt  | client.root.key | 2026/10/24 | user: root            |
```

All three types of certificates (and any related keys) are listed in the response, along with their expiry dates and accompanying notes.

The sql Command

The cockroach sql command creates a SQL shell to a CockroachDB cluster node. There are many useful subcommands to use; let's explore them now.

To connect to a CockroachDB cluster's default database, execute the following command against one of its nodes:

```
$ cockroach sql --url "postgresql://localhost?sslmode=disable"
```

This command omits the user, port, and database elements of the URL; the following command will do exactly the same as the above:

```
$ cockroach sql --url "postgresql://root@localhost:26257/
defaultdb?sslmode=disable"
```

To connect to a different database, either change the database portion of the URL or provide a -d or --database argument as follows:

```
$ cockroach sql \
    -d defaultdb \
    --url "postgresql://root@localhost:26257?sslmode=disable"
```

You may wish to run a command against a CockroachDB cluster without keeping a SQL shell open. This can be achieved with the --execute/-e argument:

```
$ cockroach sql --url "postgresql://localhost/?sslmode=disable" \
    -e "SHOW DATABASES"
  database_name | owner | primary_region | regions | survival_goal
----------------+-------+----------------+---------+---------------
  defaultdb     | root  | NULL           | {}      | NULL
  postgres      | root  | NULL           | {}      | NULL
  system        | node  | NULL           | {}      | NULL
  yo            | root  | NULL           | {}      | NULL
```

You can harness the --execute argument to perform any database operation against a cluster. It's even possible to extract data by piping the output from a statement into another command. The following statements use the --execute argument to create a table, insert data into it, and extract the data into a JSON file, all without opening a long-lived SQL shell:

```
$ cockroach sql --url "postgresql://localhost/?sslmode=disable" \
    -e "CREATE TABLE person (first_name TEXT, last_name TEXT)"

$ cockroach sql --url "postgresql://localhost/?sslmode=disable" \
    -e "INSERT INTO person (first_name, last_name) VALUES ('Ben',
'Darnell'), ('Peter', 'Mattis'), ('Spencer', 'Kimball')"

$ cockroach sql --url "postgresql://localhost/?sslmode=disable" \
    -e "SELECT first_name, last_name FROM person" --format=csv > names.csv

$ cat names.csv
first_name,last_name
Ben,Darnell
Peter,Mattis
Spencer,Kimball
```

If you'd like to watch for changes, you can pass the --watch argument in conjunction with the --execute argument. The following command will get the current database time once per second:

```
$ cockroach sql --url "postgresql://localhost/?sslmode=disable" \
```

```
  -e "SELECT NOW()" --watch 1s
                now
-------------------------------
  2021-10-31 19:45:34.878551+00
(1 row)

Time: 1ms


                now
-------------------------------
  2021-10-31 19:45:35.882499+00
(1 row)

Time: 1ms
```

The node Command

The node command provides functionality to view and manage nodes in a CockroachDB cluster. Let's create some nodes and use the node command to manage them now.

First, we'll need some nodes; create a five-node insecure cluster with the following commands (note that for the --join argument, it's enough to pass three of the five nodes, as the other nodes will get discovered via the gossip protocol):

```
$ cockroach start \
  --insecure \
  --store=node1 \
  --listen-addr=localhost:26257 \
  --http-addr=localhost:8080 \
  --join=localhost:26257,localhost:26258,localhost:26259

$ cockroach start \
  --insecure \
  --store=node2 \
  --listen-addr=localhost:26258 \
  --http-addr=localhost:8081 \
  --join=localhost:26257,localhost:26258,localhost:26259
```

```
$ cockroach start \
  --insecure \
  --store=node3 \
  --listen-addr=localhost:26259 \
  --http-addr=localhost:8082 \
  --join=localhost:26257,localhost:26258,localhost:26259

$ cockroach start \
  --insecure \
  --store=node4 \
  --listen-addr=localhost:26260 \
  --http-addr=localhost:8083 \
  --join=localhost:26257,localhost:26258,localhost:26259

$ cockroach start \
  --insecure \
  --store=node5 \
  --listen-addr=localhost:26261 \
  --http-addr=localhost:8084 \
  --join=localhost:26257,localhost:26258,localhost:26259

$ cockroach init --insecure --host=localhost:26257
```

Next, we'll use the `ls` subcommand to list our cluster nodes:

```
$ cockroach node ls --insecure
  id
------
  1
  2
  3
  4
  5
```

Next, let's get some more information from each node using the `status` subcommand. Note that because there's a lot more information being returned, I'm not using the default value for `--format` and I'm instead returning the results as records:

```
$ cockroach node status --insecure --format=records
```

```
-[ RECORD 1 ]
id           | 1
address      | localhost:26257
sql_address  | localhost:26257
build        | v21.1.7
started_at   | 2021-11-01 15:13:11.166798
updated_at   | 2021-11-01 15:15:39.681848
locality     |
is_available | true
is_live      | true
-[ RECORD 2 ]
...
```

The status subcommand provides more than just top-level information; use the following commands to expose additional node information:

- Display range information:

```
$ cockroach node status --ranges --insecure
```

- Display disk information:

```
$ cockroach node status --stats --insecure
```

- Display information relating to node state (including whether a node is training or has been decommissioned):

```
$ cockroach node status --decommission --insecure
```

- Display the combined information from the preceding commands:

```
$ cockroach node status --all --insecure
```

For each of the preceding commands, you can also display status information for individual nodes by passing a node ID as follows:

```
$ cockroach node status 1 --decommission --insecure
```

In the event that we need to take a node out of a cluster to perform maintenance, the `drain` subcommand will prevent new clients from connecting to the node and rebalance its range leases to other nodes in the cluster:

```
$ cockroach node drain --url "postgresql://localhost:26259?sslmode=disable"
```

The same can be achieved with the --host argument:

```
$ cockroach node drain --host localhost:26259 --insecure
node is draining... remaining: 4
node is draining... remaining: 0 (complete)
ok
```

Figure 4-2 shows that the node we drained is now showing as "dead" in the admin console, indicating that it is not a functioning node in the cluster anymore:

Nodes (5)

nodes ⌄	Uptime ⌄	Replicas ⌄	Capacity Usage ⌄	Memory Use ⌄	vCPUs ⌄	Version ⌄	Status ⌄	
localhost:26257 (n1)	3 minutes	35	0%	1%	8	v21.1.7	LIVE	Logs
localhost:26260 (n2)	2 minutes	36	0%	0%	8	v21.1.7	LIVE	Logs
localhost:26261 (n3)	3 minutes	35	0%	0%	8	v21.1.7	LIVE	Logs
localhost:26258 (n4)	3 minutes	36	0%	0%	8	v21.1.7	LIVE	Logs
localhost:26259 (n5)	3 minutes	36	0%	0%	8	v21.1.7	LIVE	Logs

Figure 4-2. *The Cluster Overview showing a drained node*

Once drained, a node is safe to decommission. This can be achieved with the `decommission` subcommand as follows; note that the command is followed by the ID of the node you wish to decommission:

```
$ cockroach node decommission 5 --insecure
```

The output of this command will show the replicas being reduced until there are no replicas remaining on the node. The node is then removed from the cluster and will no longer appear in the admin console.

Figure 4-3 shows how the state of the decommissioned node transitions to "DECOMMISSIONING" during the process of being decommissioned.

Nodes (5)

nodes ⇕	Uptime ⇕	Replicas ⇕	Capacity Usage ⇕	Memory Use ⇕	vCPUs ⇕	Version ⇕	Status ⇕	
localhost:26257 (n1)	5 minutes	28	0%	1%	8	v21.1.7	LIVE	Logs
localhost:26260 (n2)	5 minutes	27	0%	1%	8	v21.1.7	LIVE	Logs
localhost:26261 (n3)	5 minutes	27	0%	0%	8	v21.1.7	LIVE	Logs
localhost:26258 (n4)	5 minutes	27	0%	0%	8	v21.1.7	LIVE	Logs
localhost:26259 (n5)	5 minutes	1	0%	0%	8	v21.1.7	DECOMMISSIONING	Logs

Figure 4-3. *The Cluster Overview showing a decommissioning node*

The `recommission` subcommand can be used to recommission a node that is in the process of being decommissioned (indicated by the state of node n5 captured in Figure 4-3). If you allow a node to be fully decommissioned, it will have to be restarted, as it will no longer have permission to rejoin the cluster:

```
$ cockroach node recommission 5 --insecure
ERROR: can only recommission a decommissioning node; n5 found to be
decommissioned
Failed running "node recommission"
```

If we had terminated the decommissioning process partway through, we could issue the following command to recommission it:

```
$ cockroach node recommission 5 --insecure
```

In the event that a node is fully decommissioned, you can start the node again by first deleting its old storage directory and reissuing the start command as follows:

```
$ rm -rf node4
```

```
$ cockroach start \
  --insecure \
  --store=node4 \
  --listen-addr=localhost:26260 \
  --http-addr=localhost:8083 \
  --join=localhost:26257,localhost:26258,localhost:26259
```

The resulting node will have a new node ID, reflecting that this is not simply a recommissioning of an old node.

The `import` Command

The `import` command can be used to import small databases (<15MB) or tables from a local `pgdump` or `mysqldump` file. For anything larger than 15MB, Cockroach Labs recommends you use the `IMPORT` statement, which we'll cover in Chapter 5.

For this reason and for the symmetry of the `IMPORT`/`EXPORT` SQL statements, I prefer to use the `IMPORT`/`EXPORT` SQL statements, so will cover the exporting and importing of CockroachDB, Postgres, and MySQL files using these statements in Chapter 5.

The `sqlfmt` Command

The `sqlfmt` (pronounced "SEQUEL FUMPT") command does for SQL what the `go fmt` command does for Go code. It's useful if you'd like to format your SQL statements into a canonical format. If everyone in your team runs `sqlfmt` with the same configurations, everyone's SQL will look the same.

The `sqlfmt` command is configured with sensible defaults, so it can be used without many arguments, but I'll demonstrate these to show you how they affect the resulting SQL.

Let's pass a simple SQL command into `sqlfmt` to see how the default settings change our statement:

```
$ cockroach sqlfmt \
    -e "SELECT first_name, last_name, date_of_birth FROM person WHERE id
= '1c448ac9-73a9-47c5-9e4d-769f8aab27fd';"

SELECT
        first_name, last_name, date_of_birth
FROM
        person
WHERE
        id = '1c448ac9-73a9-47c5-9e4d-769f8aab27fd'
```

As the statement contains 160 characters (100 more than the default print width of 60), sqlfmt reformats the command so that the print width of the statement remains below 60 characters. To change the print width, pass a value to the --print-width argument.

If you prefer your SQL logic to stay on the same line as the keywords (FROM, etc.), pass the --align argument:

```
$ cockroach sqlfmt \
    -e "SELECT first_name, last_name, date_of_birth FROM person WHERE id
= '1c448ac9-73a9-47c5-9e4d-769f8aab27fd';" \
    --align

SELECT first_name, last_name, date_of_birth
  FROM person
 WHERE id = '1c448ac9-73a9-47c5-9e4d-769f8aab27fd'
```

If you SQL statement contains quotes, you can wrap it in triple quotes as follows:

```
$ cockroach sqlfmt \
    -e """SELECT p."first_name", p."last_name", p."date_of_birth",
a."name" FROM "person" p JOIN "animal" a on p.id = a."owner_id" WHERE
p."id" = '1c448ac9-73a9-47c5-9e4d-769f8aab27fd';"""
SELECT
        p.first_name, p.last_name, p.date_of_birth, a.name
FROM
        person AS p JOIN animal AS a ON p.id = a.owner_id
WHERE
        p.id = '1c448ac9-73a9-47c5-9e4d-769f8aab27fd'
```

Note that the sqlfmt command does not consider the quotes to be necessary, so it removes them before outputting the result. It will also remove other superfluous characters from the input statement such as unnecessary brackets:

```
$ cockroach sqlfmt \
    -e "SELECT first_name, last_name, date_of_birth FROM person WHERE
id IN (('1c448ac9-73a9-47c5-9e4d-769f8aab27fd'),('652cfbbc-52a9-42be-
a73f-32fc7604b7e9'));" \
    --align \
    --use-spaces
```

```
SELECT first_name, last_name, date_of_birth
  FROM person
 WHERE id
       IN (
             '1c448ac9-73a9-47c5-9e4d-769f8aab27fd',
             '652cfbbc-52a9-42be-a73f-32fc7604b7e9'
          )
```

The workload Command

The workload command generates load scenarios against a selection of databases available from the demo command. Let's create a sample database and run varying levels of load against it. Note that you don't need to start the database with the demo command to use the workload command.

First, let's start a node:

```
$ cockroach start-single-node --insecure
```

Next, we'll initialize the workload using the init subcommand:

```
$ cockroach workload init bank 'postgres://root@127.0.0.1:26257?sslmod
e=disable'
I211106 10:56:08.279758 1 workload/workloadsql/dataload.go:146  [-]
1  imported bank (0s, 1000 rows)
I211106 10:56:08.283417 1 workload/workloadsql/workloadsql.go:113  [-]
2  starting 9 splits
```

Finally, we'll start the workload with the run subcommand:

```
$ cockroach workload run bank \
      --duration=10m \
      'postgresql://root@localhost:26257?sslmode=disable'
I211106 10:56:37.308648 1 workload/cli/run.go:361  [-] 1  creating load
generator...
I211106 10:56:37.312649 1 workload/cli/run.go:392  [-] 2  creating load
generator... done (took 4.009ms)
```

```
_elapsed___errors__ops/sec(inst)___ops/sec(cum)__p50(ms)__p95(ms)__p99(ms)_
pMax(ms)
    1.0s          0              69.7
70.0      35.7      436.2        872.4      973.1 transfer
    2.0s          0             169.0
119.5     46.1      385.9       1610.6     1879.0 transfer
    3.0s          0             227.5
155.6     41.9      151.0        738.2     2281.7 transfer
    4.0s          0             247.2
178.4     44.0      159.4        805.3      872.4 transfer
...
```

Figure 4-4 shows load being generated against the bank database in the CockroachDB admin console.

Figure 4-4. *SQL Statements being executed*

By default, the load generator will run 16 concurrent workers. This can be changed depending on your requirements using the --concurrency flag. If you would like to simulate higher load, increase the concurrency.

CHAPTER 5

Interacting with CockroachDB

We've covered a lot of conceptual ground, and it's now time to start using CockroachDB as an end user. We've created clusters and tables; now, let's connect to them and put them to work.

Connecting to CockroachDB

When presented with a new database, the first thing you might want to do is connect to it and start querying! In this section, we'll connect to self-hosted and cloud-based CockroachDB clusters with tools and from code.

Connecting with Tools

There are plenty of off-the-shelf tools you can use to connect to a CockroachDB cluster. Some are free, and some you'll pay to use.

Here are some of the popular off-the-shelf tools for interacting with CockroachDB. I will be using DBeaver Community, but both DataGrip and TablePlus have excellent support for CockroachDB:

- **DBeaver** – `https://dbeaver.com`

- **DataGrip** – `www.jetbrains.com/datagrip`

- **TablePlus** – `https://tableplus.com`

© Rob Reid 2022
R. Reid, *Practical CockroachDB*, https://doi.org/10.1007/978-1-4842-8224-3_5

Let's create a CockroachDB cluster with the following command and use DBeaver to connect to it. Note that without the `--insecure` flag, CockroachDB generates a username and password. I'll use these in DBeaver. Please note that I've omitted a lot of the command output for brevity:

```
$ cockroach demo --no-example-database
# ...
#   - Connection parameters:
#     (webui)    http://127.0.0.1:8080/demologin?password=demo1892&use
#                rname=demo
#     (sql)      postgres://demo:demo1892@127.0.0.1:26257?sslmode=require
#
#   - Username: "demo", password: "demo1892"
#   - Directory with certificate files (for certain SQL drivers/tools):
#     REDACTED
# ...
demo@127.0.0.1:26257/defaultdb>
```

Now it's time to open DBeaver and connect to the database. Take note of the username and password in the preceding output. Figure 5-1 shows the configuration used to connect to this cluster using these values.

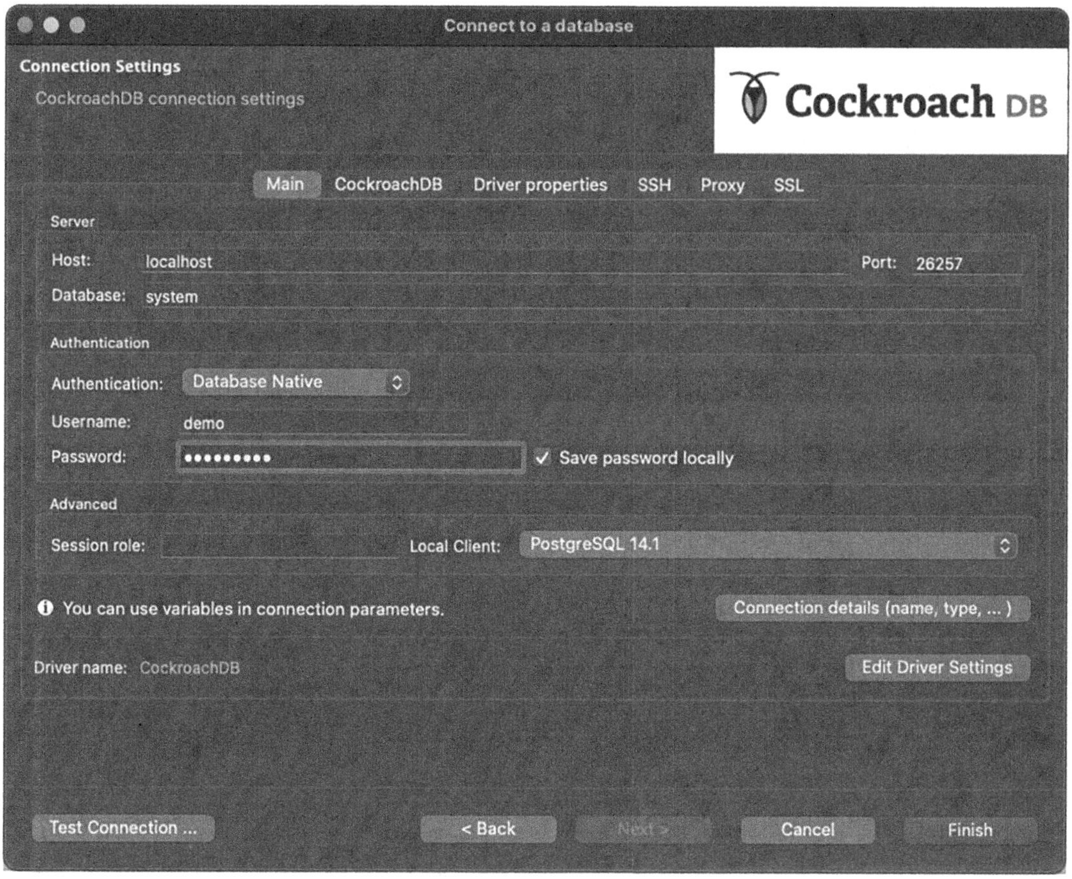

Figure 5-1. *Connection settings in DBeaver*

Note that port 26257 is the default port used by CockroachDB for database connections. As I've not altered the default port, I'm using 26257 as the connection port number here.

Now, let's create a table, insert some data into it, and select the data out to see how this looks in DBeaver. Figure 5-2 shows what working with data looks like using DBeaver.

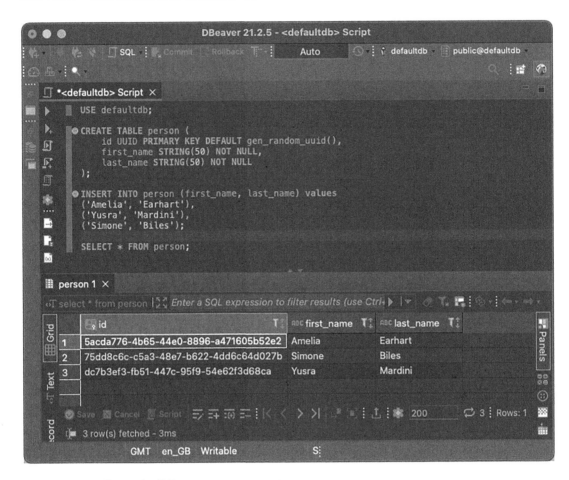

Figure 5-2. *Data in DBeaver*

The database we've connected to is basic and does not use client certificates. I'll now connect to a Cockroach Cloud database to show you how to do this with DBeaver.

Unlike a local demo database, a free-tier Cockroach Cloud database requires a certificate and an argument to tell Cockroach Cloud which cluster to connect to (it's multitenant, meaning clusters for different users are co-hosted).

Figure 5-3 shows the additional configuration values required by a Cockroach Cloud database. Namely, the host field has been updated to point to the Cockroach Cloud instance, and the database field now includes the information Cockroach Cloud requires to locate your cluster.

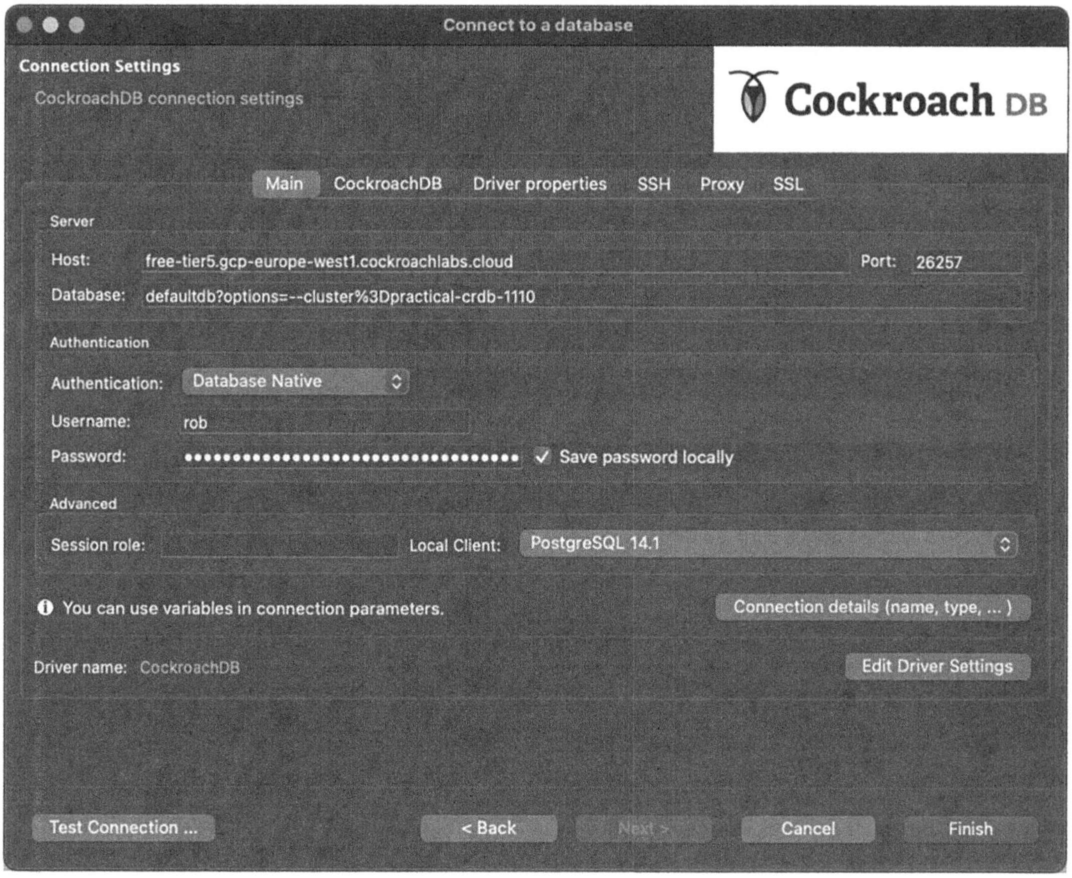

Figure 5-3. *Basic settings for connecting to a Cockroach Cloud cluster*

In addition to the basic settings, you'll need to help DBeaver find the certificate that will authenticate your connection. Figure 5-4 shows the two additional configuration values you'll need to set.

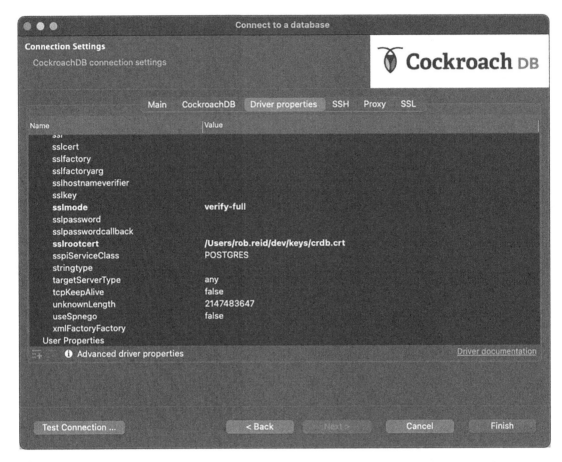

Figure 5-4. *SSL settings for connecting to a Cockroach Cloud cluster*

With these changes made, we can connect to a Cockroach Cloud database.

Connecting Programmatically

You can connect to CockroachDB from many different programming languages. Cockroach Labs lists the available drivers on their website[1] along with example applications for each.[2]

To give you a good introduction to working with CockroachDB programmatically, I'll perform some basic operations against a database using some popular drivers now.

---

[1] www.cockroachlabs.com/docs/stable/third-party-database-tools#drivers

[2] www.cockroachlabs.com/docs/stable/example-apps

Let's create a table to work with:

```
CREATE TABLE IF NOT EXISTS person (
    id UUID PRIMARY KEY DEFAULT gen_random_uuid(),
    name TEXT NOT NULL
);
```

The examples that follow show how to connect to CockroachDB and get results using several common programming languages. In each case, I've chosen succinctness over completeness in the interest of brevity.

Go Example

In this example, I'll connect to the "defaultdb" database and perform an INSERT and SELECT against the "person" table. I'll be using a popular Go driver for Postgres called pgx.

First, let's initialize the environment:

```
$ mkdir go_example
$ cd go_example
$ go mod init go_example
```

Next, we'll create a simple application in a main.go file. I'll share the key building blocks of the application here, as the complete code listing will be available on GitHub.

First, fetch and import the pgx package:

```
$ go get github.com/jackc/pgx/v4
import "github.com/jackc/pgx/v4/pgxpool"
```

Next, connect to the database and ensure that the connection is closed after use:

```
db, err := pgxpool.Connect(
            context.Background(),
            "postgres://demo:demo22992@localhost:26257/defaultdb")
if err != nil {
    log.Fatalf("error opening database connection: %v", err)
}
defer db.Close()
```

For brevity, I'm passing a `context.Context` value of `context.Background()`, which is fine for toy examples like this one. However, in scenarios where you're interacting with an actor, you'll want to pass the request context.

The pgx package does not return an error from calls to `Close()` on `*pgxpool.Pool` structs, owing to the pooled nature of the connections it manages. If you're using the `pgx.Connect()` variant of this function – which I don't recommend for multithreaded environments – you'll receive an object with a `Close()` function to call.

Suppose that instead of connecting to a local cluster, we wanted to connect to a cloud-based one; in that case, you'd pass a connection string similar to the following:

```
postgresql://<USERNAME>:<PASSWORD>@<HOST>:<PORT>/<DB_NAME>?sslmode=verify-
full&sslrootcert=<PATH_TO_CERT>&options=---cluster%3D<CLUSTER_NAME>
```

Now we're ready to insert data. The following statement inserts three names into the "people" table:

```
stmt := `INSERT INTO person (name) VALUES ($1), ($2), ($3)`
_, err = db.Exec(
    context.Background(),
    stmt,
    "Annie Easley", "Valentina Tereshkova", "Wang Zhenyi",
)
```

With the data in the table, we can now read it out:

```
stmt = `SELECT id, name FROM person`
rows, err := db.Query(context.Background(), stmt)
if err != nil {
    log.Fatalf("error querying table: %v", err)
}

var id, name string
for rows.Next() {
    if err = rows.Scan(&id, &name); err != nil {
        log.Fatalf("error reading row: %v", err)
    }
    log.Printf("%s %s", id, name)
}
```

Finally, we'll run the application using the Go toolchain:

```
$ go run main.go
2021/11/11 09:54:46 2917ee7b-3e26-4999-806a-ba799bc515b3 Wang Zhenyi
2021/11/11 09:54:46 5339cd29-77d5-4e01-966f-38ac7c6f9fbc Annie Easley
2021/11/11 09:54:46 85288df9-25fe-439a-a670-a8e8ea70c7db Valentina
Tereshkova
```

Python Example

Next, we'll create a Python application to do the same thing, connect to the "defaultdb" database, INSERT into, and SELECT out of.

First, we'll initialize the environment:

```
$ mkdir python_example
$ python3 -m pip install --no-binary :all: psycopg2
```

With the psycopg2 dependencies installed, we're ready to write our application. Let's import the dependency and create a connection to the database:

```
import psycopg2

conn = psycopg2.connect(
    dbname="defaultdb",
    user="demo",
    password="demo9315",
    port=26257,
    host="localhost",
)
```

It's a matter of preference whether you use the connect function that takes a connection string/Data Source Name (DSN) or separate variables for each of the connection elements.

Next, we'll insert some data:

```
with conn.cursor() as cur:
    cur.execute(
        "INSERT INTO person (name) VALUES (%s), (%s), (%s)",
```

```
      ('Chien-Shiung Wu', 'Lise Meitner', 'Rita Levi-Montalcini')
  )
conn.commit()
```

psycopg2's cursor function returns a cursor to use when executing statements against the database. Using the `with` statement ensures that transactions will be rolled back in the event that an exception is raised and committed if no exception is raised.

Finally, we'll read back the data we inserted:

```
with conn.cursor() as cur:
    cur.execute("SELECT id, name FROM person")
    rows = cur.fetchall()

    for row in rows:
        print(row[0], row[1])
```

psycopg2's `fetchall` command returns a list of tuples, one for each row returned. We can access the column values for each tuple by their index.

Ruby Example

Onto Ruby! Let's initialize the environment:

```
$ mkdir ruby_example
$ cd ruby_example
```

Next, we'll install the pg gem:

```
$ gem install pg
```

We're ready to create an application. First, we'll bring in the pg gem and create a connection to the database:

```
require 'pg'

conn = PG.connect(
    user: 'demo',
    password: 'demo9315',
    dbname: 'defaultdb',
    host: 'localhost',
```

```
    port: "26257",
    sslmode: 'require'
)
```

Next, let's insert some data. We'll reuse the person table:

```
conn.transaction do |tx|
    tx.exec_params(
        'INSERT INTO person (name) VALUES ($1), ($2), ($3)',
        [['Ada Lovelace'], ['Alice Ball'], ['Rosalind Franklin']],
    )
end
```

Queries that take parameters should always be parameterized. In Ruby, you pass parameters into a query using the exec_params function. I then pass a multidimensional array as a parameter, with each array containing the fields of a row to insert.

Let's read the data out. The exec/exec_params function can also be used to return data. In the following data, I pass a block into which the results of the query are available as rows. For each of the rows returned, I fetch the "id" and "name" columns:

```
conn.transaction do |tx|
    tx.exec('SELECT id, name FROM person') do |result|
        result.each do |row|
            puts row.values_at('id', 'name')
        end
    end
end
```

Finally, we'll run the application:

```
$ ruby main.rb
2bef0b0a-3b57-4f85-b0a2-58cf5f6ab7e4
["Ada Lovelace"]
5096e818-3236-4697-b919-8695fde1581d
["Rosalind Franklin"]
cf5b1f2d-f4af-4aab-8c67-3a4ced6f6c07
["Alice Ball"]
```

Crystal Example

Crystal's turn! I've been using Crystal for a number of personal projects recently (including projects backed by CockroachDB), so I wanted to make sure I covered it.

Let's prepare the environment:

```
$ crystal init app crystal_example
$ cd crystal_example
```

Next, we'll bring in a dependency that will help us communicate with CockroachDB. Open the shard.yml file and paste in the following:

```
dependencies:
  pg:
    github: will/crystal-pg
```

With the dependency in our shard files, the shards command will know what to fetch. Invoke it now to bring in our database driver:

```
$ shards install
```

In the src/crystal_example.cr file, let's connect to the database:

```
require "db"
require "pg"

db = PG.connect "postgresql://demo:demo43995@localhost:26257/
defaultdb?auth_methods=cleartext"

db.exec "INSERT INTO person (name) VALUES ($1), ($2), ($3)",
        "Florence R. Sabin", "Flossie Wong-Staal", "Marie Maynard Daly"

db.query "SELECT id, name FROM person" do |rs|
  rs.each do
    id, name = rs.read(UUID, String)
    puts "#{id} #{name}"
  end
end
```

Finally, we'll run the application:

```
$ crystal run src/crystal_example.cr
3bab85db-8ccb-4e9f-b1ba-3cf8ed1f0fc8 Florence R. Sabin
70f34efc-3c8a-4308-bdc6-dddafaccea57 Flossie Wong-Staal
cd37624f-2037-440e-b420-84a64a855792 Marie Maynard Daly
```

C# Example

Onto C#. Let's prepare the environment. For this example, I'll be using .NET 6 with C# 10:

```
$ dotnet new console --name cs_example
$ cd cs_example
```

Next, we'll bring in some NuGet package dependencies. Note that Dapper is not a required dependency for working with CockroachDB; it's just a preference in this case:

```
$ dotnet add package System.Data.SqlClient
$ dotnet add package Dapper
$ dotnet add package Npgsql
```

Now for the code. I'm omitting exception handling to keep the code succinct:

```
using Dapper;
using System.Data.SqlClient;
using Npgsql;

var connectionString = "Server=localhost:26257;Database=defaultdb;User Id=demo;Password=demo43995";

using (var connection = new NpgsqlConnection(connectionString))
{
    var people = new List<Person>()
    {
        new Person { Name = "Kamala Harris" },
        new Person { Name = "Jacinda Ardern" },
        new Person { Name = "Christine Lagarde" },
    };

    connection.Execute("INSERT INTO person (name) VALUES (@Name)", people);
```

```
foreach (var person in connection.Query<Person>("SELECT * FROM
person"))
{
    Console.WriteLine($"{person.ID} {person.Name}");
}
}

public class Person
{
    public Guid? ID { get; set; }
    public string? Name { get; set; }
}
```

Finally, we'll run the application:

```
$ dotnet run
4e363f35-4d3b-49dd-b647-7136949b1219 Christine Lagarde
5eecb866-a07f-47b4-9b45-86628864e778 Jacinda Ardern
7e466bd2-1a19-465f-9c70-9fb5f077fe79 Jacinda Ardern
```

Designing Databases

The database schemas we've designed thus far have remained purposefully simple to help demonstrate specific database features like data types. The database schemas we'll create in this section will be a more accurate reflection of what you'll create in the wild.

Database Design

We'll start by looking at CockroachDB's topmost object: the database. Up to this point, we've created tables against the defaultdb for simplicity. It's now time to create our own database.

An important decision to make before creating your database is where it will live. Will it be located in a single region, or will it span multiple regions?

If your database is to remain within a single region, it can be created as follows:

```
CREATE DATABASE db_name;
```

The preceding command will return an error if a database called "db_name" already exists. The following command will create a database only if a database with the same name does not already exist:

```
CREATE DATABASE IF NOT EXISTS db_name;
```

If your database is to span multiple regions, you'll want to provide CockroachDB with some region hints when creating your database. These include the database's primary region and any other region it is to operate within.

To demonstrate this, I'll reuse a command from an earlier chapter, which creates a CockroachDB cluster with nine nodes across three regions:

```
$ cockroach demo \
--no-example-database \
--nodes 12 \
--insecure \
--demo-locality=region=us-east1,az=a:region=us-east1,az=b:region=us-
east1,az=c:region=europe-north1,az=a:region=europe-
north1,az=b:region=europe-north1,az=c:region=europe-
west1,az=a:region=europe-west1,az=b:region=europe-west1,az=c:region=europe-
west3,az=a:region=europe-west3,az=b:region=europe-west3,az=c
```

Fetching the regions confirms that we created our expected cluster topology:

```
root@:26257/defaultdb> SHOW REGIONS;
     region     | zones   | database_names | primary_region_of
----------------+---------+----------------+--------------------
  europe-north1 | {a,b,c} | {}             | {}
  europe-west1  | {a,b,c} | {}             | {}
  europe-west3  | {a,b,c} | {}             | {}
  us-east1      | {a,b,c} | {}             | {}
```

Let's create a database that spans the European regions and see how that affects our regions view:

```
CREATE DATABASE db_name
PRIMARY REGION "europe-west1"
REGIONS = "europe-west1", "europe-west3", "europe-north1"
SURVIVE REGION failure;
root@:26257/defaultdb> SHOW REGIONS;
```

```
      region    |  zones  | database_names | primary_region_of
----------------+---------+----------------+--------------------
  europe-north1 | {a,b,c} | {db_name}      | {}
  europe-west1  | {a,b,c} | {db_name}      | {db_name}
  europe-west3  | {a,b,c} | {db_name}      | {}
  us-east1      | {a,b,c} | {}             | {}
```

The results of SHOW REGIONS confirm that our "db_name" database is running in the European regions and has a primary region of "europe-west1", just as we configured.

The SHOW REGIONS command takes additional arguments to further narrow down our search. The following command shows just the regions for the "db_name" database:

```
root@:26257/defaultdb> SHOW REGIONS FROM DATABASE db_name;
  database |    region     | primary |  zones
-----------+---------------+---------+----------
  db_name  | europe-west1  | true    | {a,b,c}
  db_name  | europe-north1 | false   | {a,b,c}
  db_name  | europe-west3  | false   | {a,b,c}
```

Schema Design

If you need to logically separate database objects such as tables, then creating a user-defined schema is a good choice. In the following example, we'll assume that we've made the decision to use user-defined schemas to logically separate our database objects. The use of custom schemas is optional. If you don't specify one yourself, the default "public" schema will be used.

In this example, we're building a database to support a simple online retail business. Supporting this online business are the following business areas:

- **Retail** – The team that builds and runs the website

- **Manufacturing** – The team that makes the products

- **Finance** – The team that manages the company accounts

In a business like this, schemas make a lot of sense, as it's feasible that each of the business areas will need an "orders" table. The retail team will need to capture customer orders, the manufacturing team will need to capture orders for raw materials, and finance would like to capture transactions made on company cards as orders.

Let's create a database with some schemas to see how we might harness schema design to give us a flexible system. First, we'll create a database:

```
CREATE DATABASE IF NOT EXISTS acme;
USE acme;
```

Next, we'll create some users to represent people in each of the three business areas:

```
CREATE USER IF NOT EXISTS retail_user;
CREATE USER IF NOT EXISTS manufacturing_user;
CREATE USER IF NOT EXISTS finance_user;
```

Finally, we'll create some schemas. The following statements create three schemas, one for each business area. For the retail and manufacturing schemas, we'll give access to the finance user, as they will need to view data from tables in both schemas:

```
CREATE SCHEMA retail AUTHORIZATION retail_user;
GRANT USAGE ON SCHEMA retail TO finance_user;

CREATE SCHEMA manufacturing AUTHORIZATION manufacturing_user;
GRANT USAGE ON SCHEMA manufacturing TO finance_user;

CREATE SCHEMA finance AUTHORIZATION finance_user;
```

With users, schemas, and grants created, let's double-check the grants using the SHOW GRANTS command:

```
SELECT schema_name, grantee, privilege_type FROM [SHOW GRANTS]
WHERE schema_name IN ('retail', 'manufacturing', 'finance')
ORDER BY 1, 2, 3;
```

```
  schema_name   |    grantee    | privilege_type
----------------+---------------+-----------------
  finance       | admin         | ALL
  finance       | root          | ALL
  manufacturing | admin         | ALL
  manufacturing | finance_user  | USAGE
  manufacturing | root          | ALL
  retail        | admin         | ALL
  retail        | finance_user  | USAGE
  retail        | root          | ALL
```

Let's connect to the database as the retail_user and create an orders table in the retail schema. Note that this is the only schema we'll be able to do this in while connected as the retail_user:

```
$ cockroach sql \
    --url "postgres://retail_user@localhost:26257/acme?sqlmode=disable" \
    --insecure
CREATE TABLE retail.orders(
    id UUID PRIMARY KEY DEFAULT gen_random_uuid(),
    reference TEXT NOT NULL
);
```

Let's do the same as the manufacturing_user:

```
$ cockroach sql \
    --url "postgres://manufacturing_user@localhost:26257/
    acme?sqlmode=disable" \
    --insecure
CREATE TABLE manufacturing.orders(
    id UUID PRIMARY KEY DEFAULT gen_random_uuid(),
    reference TEXT NOT NULL
);
```

And finally, the same again as the finance_user:

```
$ cockroach sql \
    --url "postgres://finance_user@localhost:26257/
acme?sqlmode=disable" \
    --insecure
CREATE TABLE finance.orders(
    id UUID PRIMARY KEY DEFAULT gen_random_uuid(),
    reference TEXT NOT NULL
);
```

Let's reconnect to the database as the root user and view the tables we've created:

```
$ cockroach sql \
    --url "postgres://root@localhost:26257/acme?sqlmode=disable" \
    --insecure

SELECT schema_name, table_name, owner
FROM [SHOW TABLES FROM acme];

  schema_name  | table_name |        owner
---------------+------------+---------------------
  finance      | orders     | finance_user
  manufacturing| orders     | manufacturing_user
  retail       | orders     | retail_user
```

Table Design

There are plenty of considerations to make when creating tables in any database, and CockroachDB is no exception. Among other things, badly named columns, incorrect use of data types, missing (or redundant) indexes, and badly configured primary keys can hurt readability and performance.

In this section, we'll take a look at some table design best practices.

Naming

It's important to know where CockroachDB will create a table, so it's vitally important that you provide a name that instructs CockroachDB exactly where to place it.

Where do you think CockroachDB will place the following table?

```
CREATE TABLE table_name();
```

If you said any variation of ¯_(ツ)_/¯, you're not far off. The following outcomes could result:

- The table exists in the public schema of whichever database you currently have selected.

- The table exists in the public schema of the defaultdb database.

- You receive an error asking you to select a database.

In short, creating a table like this is ill-advised when working with production-scale systems. Providing the fully qualified name of the table is so important. In the following example, we've removed any uncertainty about where the table should live:

```
CREATE TABLE database_name.schema_name.table_name();
```

Always give your tables descriptive names. The choice of singular vs. plural table names and whether you decide to PascalCase, camelCase, snake_case, or SPoNgEBOb case is yours to make. However, whatever you decide, it's always a good idea to remain consistent with your naming convention.

Column Data Types

CockroachDB has many column types, and to get the best out of your database, you'll need to know when to use them and when not to use them.

Take the following table, for example. Other than my purposeful inclusion of two role-based columns, age specified as an integer and not timestamp, and omission of a database and schema, how many questionable design decisions can you spot?

```
CREATE TABLE users (
    id SERIAL PRIMARY KEY,
    name STRING,
    age INT,
    is_admin INT,
    primary_role STRING
);
```

Here's a list of potential issues I can identify in the design of this table:

- Every column, except for the ID column, is nullable.

- The ID column uses the SERIAL data type, which only exists for Postgres compatibility. In most scenarios, it's better to use the UUID data type, whose values distribute more evenly across ranges.

- The length of the name and primary_role columns is not limited.

- The age column can store values between -9,223,372,036,854,775,807 and +9,223,372,036,854,775,807, which, given our current scientific progress, seems unlikely.

- The is_admin column can also store a large number, but the main problem with this column being of type INT is that there exists a better data type to convey the Boolean semantics of this column: BOOL.

- An ENUM data type for the primary_role column may better fit, given we'd have a finite range of values.

Here's the table again but this time, with the issues I've identified resolved:

```
CREATE TYPE users_primary_role AS ENUM (
    'admin',
    'write',
    'read'
);

CREATE TABLE users (
    id UUID PRIMARY KEY DEFAULT gen_random_uuid(),
    name STRING(50) NOT NULL,
    age INT2 NOT NULL,
    is_admin BOOL NOT NULL DEFAULT false,
    primary_role users_primary_role NOT NULL DEFAULT 'read'
);
```

In summary:

- There's usually a data type that is well suited to the data you'd like to store.

- If you can make some reasonable predictions to the amount of data in a column, use the limited variable-length variant of a data type where possible.

- If you require data in a given column, make it nonnullable.

- Use ENUMs to represent the choice between a finite set of string values.

- Consider using DEFAULT values to achieve Least Privilege semantics.

Indexes

Use indexes to improve the performance of SELECT queries by giving CockroachDB hints as to where it should look in a dataset for the value(s) you're requesting.

CockroachDB distinguishes between two types of indexes:

- **Primary indexes** – Every table receives a primary index. If you have provided a primary key for a table, this will be your table's primary index. If you have not provided an index, CockroachDB will create a primary index called "rowid" and assign a unique value to each row.

- **Secondary indexes** – Secondary indexes are used to improve the performance of SELECT queries and are recommended for any column you will be filtering on or sorting in your queries.

In the following example, I'm creating a table with no primary or secondary indexes:

```
CREATE TABLE person (
    id UUID NOT NULL DEFAULT gen_random_uuid(),
    date_of_birth TIMESTAMP NOT NULL,
    pets STRING[]
);
```

Let's run a query to see how our table looks like in CockroachDB:

```
SELECT column_name, column_default, is_nullable, data_type
FROM defaultdb.information_schema.columns
WHERE table_name = 'person';
```

column_name	column_default	is_nullable	data_type
id	gen_random_uuid()	NO	uuid
date_of_birth	NULL	NO	timestamp without time zone
pets	NULL	YES	ARRAY
rowid	unique_rowid()	NO	bigint

As you can see from the aforementioned, CockroachDB has generated a fourth column called rowid as a substitute for our missing primary key column. Values for this column are auto-incrementing but not necessarily sequential. As can be seen with a call to unique_rowid():

```
SELECT abs(unique_rowid() - unique_rowid()) AS difference;

  difference
--------------
     32768
```

To see what CockroachDB has generated for us, I'll run another command to generate the table's CREATE statement:

```
SHOW CREATE TABLE person;

  table_name |                          create_statement
-------------+-----------------------------------------------------------------
  person     | CREATE TABLE public.person (
             |       id UUID NOT NULL DEFAULT gen_random_uuid(),
             |       date_of_birth TIMESTAMP NOT NULL,
             |       pets STRING[] NULL,
             |       rowid INT8 NOT VISIBLE NOT NULL DEFAULT unique_rowid(),
             |       CONSTRAINT "primary" PRIMARY KEY (rowid ASC),
             |       FAMILY "primary" (id, date_of_birth, pets, rowid)
             | )
```

Let's create the table again but this time, provide a primary key of our own:

```
CREATE TABLE person (
    id UUID PRIMARY KEY DEFAULT gen_random_uuid(),
    date_of_birth TIMESTAMP NOT NULL,
    pets STRING[]
);
```

Now that the ID column in our table is the primary key, CockroachDB has not created its own primary key for us:

```
SELECT column_name, column_default, is_nullable, data_type
FROM defaultdb.information_schema.columns
WHERE table_name = 'person';
```

column_name	column_default	is_nullable	data_type
id	gen_random_uuid()	NO	uuid
date_of_birth	NULL	NO	timestamp without time zone
pets	NULL	YES	ARRAY

With the table in place, let's insert some data into it and see how CockroachDB searches the table when queried:

```
INSERT INTO person (date_of_birth, pets) VALUES
('1980-01-01', ARRAY['Mittens', 'Fluffems']),
('1979-02-02', NULL),
('1996-03-03', ARRAY['Mr. Dog']),
('2001-04-04', ARRAY['His Odiousness, Lord Dangleberry']),
('1954-05-05', ARRAY['Steve']);

EXPLAIN SELECT id, date_of_birth FROM person
WHERE date_of_birth BETWEEN '1979-01-01' and '1997-12-31'
AND pets <@ ARRAY['Mr. Dog']
ORDER BY date_of_birth;

  distribution: full
  vectorized: true

  • sort
  │ estimated row count: 0
  │ order: +date_of_birth
  │
  └── • filter
      │ estimated row count: 0
      │ filter: ((date_of_birth >= '1979-01-01 00:00:00') AND (date_of_
birth <= '1997-12-31 00:00:00')) AND (pets <@ ARRAY['Mr. Dog'])
      │
      └── • scan
```

```
estimated row count: 5 (100% of the table; stats collected 5
minutes ago)
table: person@primary
spans: FULL SCAN
```

Uh oh! CockroachDB has had to perform a full scan of the entire person table to fulfill our query. Queries will get linearly slower with every new row added to the database.

Secondary indexes to the rescue! Let's recreate the table with indexes on the columns we'll filter and sort on. In our case, that's the date_of_birth and the pets column:

```
CREATE TABLE person (
    id UUID PRIMARY KEY DEFAULT gen_random_uuid(),
    date_of_birth TIMESTAMP NOT NULL,
    pets STRING[],

    INDEX (date_of_birth),
    INVERTED INDEX (pets)
);

EXPLAIN SELECT id, date_of_birth FROM person
WHERE date_of_birth BETWEEN '1979-01-01' and '1997-12-31'
AND pets <@ ARRAY['Mr. Dog']
ORDER BY date_of_birth;

  distribution: local
  vectorized: true

  • filter
  │ filter: pets <@ ARRAY['Mr. Dog']
  │
  └── • index join
      │ table: person@primary
      │
      └── • scan
            missing stats
            table: person@person_date_of_birth_idx
            spans: [/'1979-01-01 00:00:00' - /'1997-12-31 00:00:00']
```

107

Success! Our query no longer requires a full table scan. Note what happens, however, if we order the results in descending order of date_of_birth:

```
EXPLAIN SELECT id, date_of_birth FROM person
WHERE date_of_birth BETWEEN '1979-01-01' and '1997-12-31'
AND pets <@ ARRAY['Mr. Dog']
ORDER BY date_of_birth DESC;

  distribution: full
  vectorized: true

  • sort
  │ order: -date_of_birth
  │
  └── • filter
      │ filter: pets <@ ARRAY['Mr. Dog']
      │
      └── • index join
          │ table: person@primary
          │
          └── • scan
              missing stats
              table: person@person_date_of_birth_idx
              spans: [/'1979-01-01 00:00:00' - /'1997-12-31 00:00:00']
```

CockroachDB has had to sort the results manually for us before returning them because the indexes on the table sort in ascending order by default and we've asked for them in descending order.

Suppose you know that CockroachDB may return the results of a query in either ascending or descending order by a column. In that case, it's worth considering adding indexes for both scenarios as follows:

```
CREATE TABLE person (
    id UUID PRIMARY KEY DEFAULT gen_random_uuid(),
    date_of_birth TIMESTAMP NOT NULL,
    pets STRING[],

    INDEX person_date_of_birth_asc_idx (date_of_birth ASC),
```

```
    INDEX person_date_of_birth_desc_idx (date_of_birth DESC),
    INVERTED INDEX (pets)
);
```

With this in place, CockroachDB knows how to return query results that are ordered by date_of_birth in ascending or descending order without having to manually sort them.

If you're indexing columns containing sequential data, such as TIMESTAMP or incrementing INT values, you may want to consider using hash-sharded indexes.[3] Hash-sharded indexes ensure that indexed data is distributed evenly across ranges, which prevent single-range hotspots. Single-range hotspots occur when multiple similar values are queried and exist in the same range.

At the time of writing, hash-sharded indexes are still experimental, so they need to be enabled as follows:

```
SET experimental_enable_hash_sharded_indexes = true;

CREATE TABLE device_event (
    device_id UUID NOT NULL,
    event_timestamp TIMESTAMP NOT NULL,
    INDEX (device_id, event_timestamp) USING HASH WITH bucket_count = 10
);
```

Under the covers, the values in the index will be an FNV hash representation of the data you're indexing. Any small changes to the input data may result in a different hash output and a different index bucket. The table can now scale more evenly across the nodes in your cluster, resulting in increased performance.

View Design

A view is simply a SELECT query that you assign a name to ask CockroachDB to remember. CockroachDB supports three types of views:

- **Materialized views** – CockroachDB stores the resulting data for improved performance in subsequent queries. I would only recommend using materialized views if you cannot index the data in

---

[3] www.cockroachlabs.com/docs/stable/hash-sharded-indexes

your table, for query performance, and if the data in that table does not update frequently. If data frequently updates, your results might be stale.

- **Dematerialized views** – The results of a view are not stored, meaning data is always consistent with the table. As the results are not stored, CockroachDB will query the underlying table for each view query. If you've appropriately indexed your table for performance, dematerialized views are the best choice, as they will always return correct data.

- **Temporary views** – Temporary views are ephemeral views that are accessible only to the session in which they were created and deleted at the end of that session.

If you need to restrict table data to specific users or have complex queries you'd like to expose as simpler ones, views are a good choice. Let's create some views to see what they can offer us.

Simplify Queries

Suppose you have a query whose complexity you'd like to hide (or simply not have to rewrite). You can create a view over this data to expose a simpler query.

Let's assume we're running an online shop and would like a query to return the number of purchases by day. Granted, this is a straightforward query, but for the sake of argument, we'll wrap this in a view to demonstrate the concept.

First, we'll create the tables:

```
CREATE TABLE customer (
    id UUID PRIMARY KEY DEFAULT gen_random_uuid(),
    email STRING(50) NOT NULL,

    INDEX(email)
);

CREATE TABLE product (
    id UUID PRIMARY KEY DEFAULT gen_random_uuid(),
    sku STRING(20) NOT NULL,
```

```
        INDEX(sku)
);

CREATE TABLE purchase (
        customer_id UUID NOT NULL REFERENCES customer(id),
        product_id UUID NOT NULL REFERENCES product(id),
        checkout_at TIMESTAMPTZ NOT NULL
);
```

Next, we'll insert some data into the tables to give us something to work with:

```
INSERT INTO customer (email) VALUES
('m.curie@gmail.com'),
('l.meitner@gmail.com'),
('d.hodgkin@gmail.com');

INSERT INTO product (sku) VALUES
('E81ML1GA'),
('4UXK19DO'),
('L28COXJ4');

INSERT INTO purchase (customer_id, product_id, checkout_at) VALUES
('2df28d7d-67a3-4e83-a713-96a68a196b0b', '486ecc02-6d8e-44fe-b8ef-
b8d004658465', '2021-11-23T06:50:46Z'),
('5047d78c-12cc-48e3-a36a-7cac1018ba7e', '5b2756e6-
cc88-47e6-849d-6291a76f3881', '2021-11-22T08:13:13+07:00'),
('792ab188-1bb2-4ac6-b1d2-f1adbcf9223e', '6cfd7bed-
bf11-4c96-9300-82c8e9dd97f2', '2021-11-23T06:50:46-05:00');
```

Finally, we'll create the view. This view will be a simple selection on the purchase table, along with a grouping over the extracted day-of-week value of the checkout_ at column:

```
CREATE VIEW purchases_by_dow (dow, purchases) AS
SELECT EXTRACT('ISODOW', pu.checkout_at), COUNT(*)
FROM purchase pu
GROUP BY EXTRACT('ISODOW', pu.checkout_at);
```

With this in place, we can now work against the view, which hides the complexity of the date manipulation:

```
SELECT * FROM purchases_by_dow;
  dow | purchases
------+------------
    2 |          2
    1 |          1
```

Restrict Table Data

Another good use case for views is for restricting access to data. In the following example, we'll create a table and restrict its data to groups of users.

Assume that in the previous example, our shop operates globally. We might not want to sell all products everywhere, so limiting the products we show users in different countries makes sense.

Before we begin, we'll need to create and connect to a secure cluster. Let's create a single-node cluster now.

```
$ mkdir certs
$ mkdir keys

$ cockroach cert create-ca \
    --certs-dir=certs \
    --ca-key=keys/ca.key

$ cockroach cert create-node \
    --certs-dir=certs \
    --ca-key=keys/ca.key \
    localhost

$ cockroach start-single-node \
    --certs-dir=certs \
    --store=node1 \
    --listen-addr=localhost:26257 \
    --http-addr=localhost:8080
```

```
$ cockroach cert create-client \
    root \
    --certs-dir=certs \
    --ca-key=keys/ca.key
```

```
$ cockroach sql --certs-dir=certs
```

First, we'll create the products table and insert some products into it:

```
CREATE TABLE product (
    id UUID PRIMARY KEY DEFAULT gen_random_uuid(),
    country_iso STRING(3) NOT NULL,
    sku STRING(20) NOT NULL
);
```

```
INSERT INTO product (country_iso, sku) VALUES
('BRA', 'E81ML1GA'),
('FIN', '4UXK19DO'),
('GBR', 'L28COXJ4');
```

Next, we'll create a view to return all products for customers in the UK:

```
CREATE VIEW product_gbr (id, country_iso, sku) AS
SELECT id, country_iso, sku FROM product
WHERE country_iso = 'GBR';
```

Finally, we'll create a user and grant them access to the view. We'll assume the following user will serve UK customers:

```
CREATE USER user_gbr WITH LOGIN PASSWORD 'some_password';
```

```
GRANT SELECT ON product_gbr TO user_gbr;
REVOKE SELECT ON product FROM user_gbr;
```

Let's connect to the database as the new user and see what we can (and can't) access:

```
$ cockroach sql \
    --certs-dir=certs \
    --url "postgres://user_gbr:some_password@localhost:26257/defaultdb"
```

```
user_gbr@localhost:26257/defaultdb> SELECT * FROM product;
ERROR: user user_gbr does not have SELECT privilege on relation product
SQLSTATE: 42501

user_gbr@localhost:26257/defaultdb> SELECT * FROM product_gbr;
                 id                  | country_iso |    sku
-------------------------------------+-------------+-----------
  d1c055ed-1a2e-4383-875e-3c53a2bf65cc | GBR         | L28C0XJ4
```

We're in business! Our user_gbr user has no access to query the product table directly but *does* have access to its data via the product_gbr view, which exposes only the products we'd like them to see.

Moving Data

In this section, we'll explore some use cases that involve moving data into and out of databases via the IMPORT and EXPORT statements and CDC (Change Data Capture).

Exporting and Importing Data

Unless you're creating a new database to store new data, you'll likely need to migrate data from another database. This section will show you how to export data out of and import data into CockroachDB tables.

To start, let's create a single-node cluster:

```
$ cockroach demo --no-example-database --insecure
```

With a cluster in place, we'll create a database with two tables: one table to export data out of and another table to import data into. We'll also insert some data to export:

```
CREATE DATABASE import_export;
USE import_export;

CREATE TABLE to_export (
  name TEXT NOT NULL
);

CREATE TABLE to_import (
```

```
  name TEXT NOT NULL
);
```

```
INSERT INTO to_export (name) VALUES ('A'), ('B'), ('C');
```

Next, we'll need somewhere to export our data. CockroachDB supports cloud provider destinations such as Amazon S3, Azure Storage, and Google Cloud Storage and allows you to export to self-hosted destinations.

For this example, I've created a basic HTTP server that I'm hosting in replit.com under https://replit.com/@robreid/importexport. You can sign up for a free Replit account and fork this Repl to test your own exports/imports.

With a server up and running and available at https://importexport.robreid. repl.co, I can export data as follows (you will have a different URL in the form of https://importexport.YOUR_USERNAME.repl.co):

```
EXPORT INTO CSV 'https://importexport.robreid.repl.co'
FROM TABLE to_export;

                              filename
| rows | bytes
-------------------------------------------------------------------+-----
-+-------
  export16b4ae42664118980000000000000001-n707964976657694721.0.csv
|    3 |      6
```

We can confirm that the file has been successfully ingested by the server but joining the address of the running Repl with the file name in the preceding response:

```
$ curl https://importexport.robreid.repl.co/export16b4ae42664118980000000
000000001-n707964976657694721.0.csv
A
B
C
```

Let's import this data into our "to_import" table now:

```
IMPORT INTO to_import (name)
    CSV DATA (
```

```
  'https://importexport.robreid.repl.co/export16b4ae426641189800000000
  00000001-n707964976657694721.0.csv'
);
```

```
    job_id        | status  | fraction_completed | rows |
index_entries | bytes
--------------------+-----------+--------------------+------+
---------------+-------
707965889435041793 | succeeded |                  1 |    3 |
            0 |    60
```

CockroachDB also supports importing data from Avro files, TSV and other delimited files, and CockroachDB, MySQL, and Postgres dump files. I recommend using the IMPORT statement in the following scenarios:

- You need to insert a lot of data quickly.

- You need to insert data outside of your application's typical insert workflow. In this instance, having a process for importing data from files might make sense.

Watching for Database Changes

Like Postgres, CockroachDB supports Change Data Capture (CDC), which allows you to stream changes to table data out of CockroachDB and into external systems.

In this section, we'll create an Enterprise Changefeed and stream data changes out of a table. Changefeeds are available in both Enterprise and Core clusters, but the creation syntax and behaviors are slightly different.

Kafka Sink

The Kafka CDC sink was the first to appear in CockroachDB, making its first appearance in v2.1.

In this example, I'll use Redpanda, a streaming platform that's wire-compatible with Kafka (in the same way that CockroachDB is wire-compatible with Postgres). Let's start an instance of Redpanda, create a topic, and consume from it:

```
$ docker run \
    --rm -it \
```

```
    --name redpanda \
    -p 9092:9092 \
    -p 9644:9644 \
    docker.vectorized.io/vectorized/redpanda:latest \
    redpanda start \
        --overprovisioned \
        --smp 1  \
        --memory 1G \
        --reserve-memory OM \
        --node-id 0 \
        --check=false

$ docker exec -it \
    redpanda rpk topic create cdc_example \
        --brokers=localhost:9092

$ docker exec -it \ .
    redpanda rpk topic consume cdc_example \
        --brokers=localhost:9092
```

Moving back to Cockroach, let's create a simple insecure demo cluster with an example table to stream data from:

```
$ cockroach demo --no-example-database --insecure
CREATE TABLE example (
    id UUID PRIMARY KEY DEFAULT gen_random_uuid(),
    value STRING(10) NOT NULL
);
```

With the table in place, let's create a Kafka Changefeed to start publishing changes:

```
SET CLUSTER SETTING kv.rangefeed.enabled = true;

CREATE CHANGEFEED FOR TABLE example
INTO 'kafka://localhost:9092?topic_name=cdc_example'
WITH updated;
```

Note that in order to create a Changefeed for multiple tables, simply provide a comma-separated string containing the tables you'd like to monitor as follows:

```
CREATE CHANGEFEED FOR TABLE table_one, table_two, table_three
INTO 'kafka://localhost:9092?topic_name=cdc_example'
WITH updated;
```

The only thing required to get data into Kafka now is to use your tables as normal. All changes to the data in our example table will be automatically published to Kafka. Let's INSERT, UPDATE, and DELETE some data now and see what CockroachDB publishes to the cdc_example topic:

```
INSERT INTO example (value) VALUES ('a');

UPDATE example
SET value = 'b'
WHERE id = '4c0ebb98-7f34-436e-9f6b-7ea1888327d9';

DELETE FROM example
WHERE id = '4c0ebb98-7f34-436e-9f6b-7ea1888327d9';
```

You'll start to see the events received from CockroachDB via the Redpanda consumer at this point. The first message received represents the change introduced by the INSERT statement, the second message was published after the UPDATE statement, and the last message shows the row being deleted as a result of the DELETE statement:

```
{
  "topic": "cdc_example",
  "key": "[\"4c0ebb98-7f34-436e-9f6b-7ea1888327d9\"]",
  "value": "{\"after\": {\"id\": \"4c0ebb98-7f34-436e-9f6b-7ea1888327d9\",
\"value\": \"a\"}, \"updated\": \"1637755793947605000.0000000000\"}",
  "timestamp": 1637755794706,
  "partition": 0,
  "offset": 44
}
{
  "topic": "cdc_example",
  "key": "[\"4c0ebb98-7f34-436e-9f6b-7ea1888327d9\"]",
  "value": "{\"after\": {\"id\": \"4c0ebb98-7f34-436e-9f6b-7ea1888327d9\",
\"value\": \"b\"}, \"updated\": \"1637755826616641000.0000000000\"}",
  "timestamp": 1637755826791,
  "partition": 0,
```

```
  "offset": 45
}
{
  "topic": "cdc_example",
  "key": "[\"4c0ebb98-7f34-436e-9f6b-7ea1888327d9\"]",
  "value": "{\"after\": null, \"updated\": \"163775601102495500
  0.0000000000\"}",
  "timestamp": 1637756011195,
  "partition": 0,
  "offset": 46
}
```

To stop a Changefeed, you need to locate and delete the job that's running it. Let's find the job and cancel it now:

```
root@127.0.0.1:26257/defaultdb> SELECT job_id, job_type, description FROM
[SHOW JOBS];

        job_id       |  job_type  |               description
---------------------+------------+-----------------------------------------
  713311406086291457 | CHANGEFEED | CREATE CHANGEFEED FOR TABLE example
INTO 'kafka://localhost:9092?topic_name=cdc_example' WITH updated

root@127.0.0.1:26257/defaultdb> CANCEL JOB 713311406086291457;
```

Webhook Sink

Let's redirect our CDC events to a web server now. Owing to the potentially sensitive nature of the data in your tables, CockroachDB will only send data to HTTPS-enabled servers. Like the previous export/import example, I'll reuse replit.com to create and run a free HTTPS server. Let's create and run a simple HTTPS server:

```
package main

import (
    "io/ioutil"
    "log"
    "net/http"
)
```

```go
func main() {
    http.HandleFunc("/", cdc)
    log.Fatal(http.ListenAndServe(":9090", nil))
}

func cdc(w http.ResponseWriter, r *http.Request) {
    defer func() {
        if err := r.Body.Close(); err != nil {
            log.Printf("error closing request body: %v", err)
        }
    }()

    event, err := ioutil.ReadAll(r.Body)
    if err != nil {
        log.Printf("error reading request body: %v", err)
    }

    log.Println(string(event))
}
```

Feel free to fork my Repl at https://replit.com/@robreid/cdcexample.

Copy the URL of your running server (mine is https://cdcexample.robreid.repl.co) and plug it into CockroachDB to start publishing webhook CDC events:

```sql
CREATE CHANGEFEED FOR TABLE example
INTO 'webhook-https://cdcexample.robreid.repl.co?insecure_tls_skip_
verify=true'
WITH updated;
```

Finally, let's generate some events with INSERT, UPDATE, and DELETE statements:

```sql
INSERT INTO example (value) VALUES ('b');

UPDATE example SET value = 'b'
WHERE id = 'aea98953-0a9b-4315-a55f-e95bc7dc8305';

DELETE FROM example
WHERE id = 'aea98953-0a9b-4315-a55f-e95bc7dc8305';
```

Switching back to replit.com, our server is now receiving events for CockroachDB changes:

2021/11/24 12:41:13 {"payload":[{"after":{"id":"aea98953-0a9b-4315-a55f-e95bc7dc8305","value":"b"},"key":["aea98953-0a9b-4315-a55f-e95bc7dc8305"]," topic":"example","updated":"1637757672559012000.0000000000"}],"length":1}

2021/11/24 12:41:20 {"payload":[{"after":{"id":"aea98953-0a9b-4315-a55f-e95bc7dc8305","value":"b"},"key":["aea98953-0a9b-4315-a55f-e95bc7dc8305"]," topic":"example","updated":"1637757679279445000.0000000000"}],"length":1}

2021/11/24 12:41:20 {"payload":[{"after":null,"key":["aea98953-0a9b-4315-a55f-e95bc7dc8305"],"topic":"example","updated":"1637757680248432000.0000 000000"}],"length":1}

## CHAPTER 6

Data Privacy

Data privacy should be a concern for businesses great and small, regardless of where they are in the world. While the laws affecting the penalties for poorly implemented security can vary from country to country, the safeguarding of users is of paramount importance.

In this topic, we'll take a closer look at how CockroachDB can support you in creating a secure and compliant infrastructure for your data.

Global Regulations

There is no one data privacy law that governs the entire world. Each country has its own legislation, which it can revise over time. This makes for a forever-changing landscape that we as engineers need to keep up and remain compliant with. The DLA Piper law firm maintains an excellent site that provides a country-by-country overview of this landscape: `www.dlapiperdataprotection.com`. I will be using DLA Piper's research as my starting point for the content in this section.

What I present in this section should not be considered legal advice. Before creating a production CockroachDB cluster for customer data, please consult a data privacy specialist.

Here are a few headlines to give you a sense of the complexity of this compliance challenge:

- There is no documented standard by which data can be globally considered subject to protection. In some heavily regulated countries, the definition of Personally Identifiable Information (PII) is well defined, whereas in other heavily regulated countries, it is not defined at all.

- In the United States, the devolution of data privacy legislative power to each state means every state can have different data privacy laws.

R. Reid, *Practical CockroachDB*, https://doi.org/10.1007/978-1-4842-8224-3_6

- The California Consumer Privacy Act (CCPA) is now in effect, making it the first comprehensive state-wide privacy policy. While often compared to Europe's General Data Protection Regulation (GDPR), the two differ in subtle but important ways; the GDPR framework requires "prior consent" from individuals, whereas the CCPA framework gives individuals the right to "opt out."[1]

- The GDPR sets the age of consent for data collection and processing at 16 but allows European member states to lower that if they wish. As a result, there is no one definition of a child regarding data protection in Europe.[2]

- Following Brexit, the UK has created a UK-specific GDPR, which is, for the most part, the same as the EU equivalent. However, some parts of the UK's Data Protection Act 2018 (DPA) affect those provided by the GDPR.

- There is no standard definition for what can be considered a data transfer in Europe. As a result, everything that touches data is considered a transfer.

The list of regulations and their differences is beyond the scope of this book. However, I hope that by sharing the preceding points, I've highlighted the importance of understanding the data privacy laws in any country where you are operating or from which you will have users whose data you will collect or process.

Your responsibilities and liabilities will change, depending on whether you are considered a processor, a controller, or a joint controller of data, so it's important to understand the difference between the two. In the UK, the Information Commissioner's Office (ICO) has a useful checklist to help you identify your role.[3] In short, however, if you have decided to collect data and know how and why you are processing it, you are a controller.

---

[1] www.cookiebot.com/en/ccpa-vs-gdpr-compliance-with-cookiebot-cmp

[2] www.clarip.com/data-privacy/gdpr-child-consent

[3] https://ico.org.uk/for-organisations/guide-to-data-protection/guide-to-the-general-data-protection-regulation-gdpr/key-definitions/controllers-and-processors/

Your responsibilities and liabilities will also change depending on the type of data you are processing. If you store healthcare data (e.g., patient names and health conditions), you will be subject to more scrutiny than if you store customer data (e.g., customer email and physical addresses) in an online retail setting.

As a rule of thumb, if you are operating across multiple countries, it's wise to comply with the country with the most stringent data privacy laws and apply this across all countries. Additionally, if two countries have conflicting rules, you may need to implement rules for each country on a customer-by-customer basis, depending on their home country/state.

Although navigating the complex waters of data privacy remains an important consideration for all database users, CockroachDB's encryption in transit, encryption at rest, and geo-partitioning functionally make the complexity easier to manage.

Location-Specific Considerations

In this section, we'll take a closer look at the considerations you'll need to make when operating across geographies and under different circumstances that will affect your compliance responsibilities.

UK Company with UK and European Customers

If you are a UK-based company and have customers in the UK and the EU, you will be subject to GDPR and UK-GDPR. Following Brexit, the UK adopted all of the principles of the original GDPR framework, meaning that if you satisfy GDPR, you'll be compliant in both the EU and the UK.

On June 28, 2021, the European Commission acknowledged that the personal data of European citizens could be safely stored in the UK via two adequacy decisions.[4] As a result, you are free to store data either in the UK or the EU. As personal data can flow freely into and out of the UK, you have flexibility as to how your cluster is architected:

- **Process all customer data in the UK** – To keep your infrastructure costs and complexity down, you could run your cluster within a single region in the UK. Owing to the proximity of the UK to the rest of Europe, latencies to central Europe will be between 12ms and 33ms depending on your cloud provider. Visit `www.cloudping.co/grid` for a latency grid for AWS regions.

---

[4] `https://ec.europa.eu/commission/presscorner/detail/en/ip_21_3183`

- **Process all customer data in the EU** – For the same reason that housing all data within a single UK region will keep costs down and infrastructure simple, housing all data within a single EU region can also be a good option.

- **One cluster with nodes close to your users** – CockroachDB's ability to scale horizontally across regions would work well in this scenario. You can create a cluster of database nodes across multiple regions and place nodes near your customers, wherever they are in the UK or Europe.

European Company with European and American Customers

If you are a Europe-based company and have customers in Europe and the United States, you will be subject to both GDPR and the states' regulations in which you have customers in the United States.

As GDPR is currently more restrictive than any US data privacy framework (including CCPA), applying GDPR for both your European and US customers could make sense.

You have three main options regarding the location of stored data:

- **Process all customer data in Europe** – Schrems II protects Europeans from US government surveillance, so storing US customer data in EU data centers is more straightforward than storing EU customer data in US data centers. The obvious drawback of this approach is the latency US customers will face if their requests are hitting EU database nodes directly.

- **One cluster with geographically separated nodes** – If you'd like to run a single, multiregion cluster, you could use geo-partitioning to separate EU and US customer data.

- **Multiple isolated clusters** – If you'd rather keep EU and US customer data completely isolated, you could run two clusters: one in the EU and one in the United States.

Each of these options has benefits and trade-offs. I would either run a single geo-partitioned cluster or multiple isolated clusters in this scenario.

American Company with American Customers

If you are a US-based company with just US customers, you'll need to consider the various state regulations around the country.

At the time of writing, there are three comprehensive frameworks in use in the United States: CCPA, VCDPA, and ColoPA for customers in California, Virginia, and Colorado, respectively. Each framework provides a different level of protection for customers. For example, VCDPA received input from Amazon and so works for businesses rather than customers.[5]

As with the EU/US example, rather than trying to achieve compliance with a growing number of very different data privacy frameworks, it makes sense to aim for compliance with the most restrictive framework. We've identified that VCDPA is not a customer-centric framework, so we know that CCPA will be the more restrictive framework, but what about ColoPA? CCPA gives customers *some* ability to sue companies over negligence concerning data handling, but ColoPA offers no such ability.

Applying CCPA for customers outside of California makes sense for the same reason that applying GDPR for US customers makes sense; it's the more restrictive data privacy framework.

American Company with American and European Customers

On July 16, 2020, Schrems II came into effect.[6] It found the possibility of US government surveillance under the Foreign Intelligence Surveillance Act (FISA) a sufficient enough threat to the data privacy of EU citizens to invalidate the EU-US Data Protection Shield that had been in place.

As a result, a US company wishing to store data on EU customers must comply with GDPR legislation. In this knowledge, it would be wise to separate US and EU customer data in this scenario. If we need to do any analytical processing of the data in the United States, it would be acceptable to take an anonymized copy of EU customer data and store that in the United States.

---

[5] www.nytimes.com/wirecutter/blog/state-of-privacy-laws-in-us
[6] www.brabners.com/blogs/why-does-it-matter-which-country-i-store-my-data

There are many ways we could design a compliant database infrastructure for this scenario. Let's review two options:

- **Multiple isolated clusters** – This is the safest way to operate in this scenario, as cluster information, credentials, and certificates remain separate.

- **One cluster with geographically separated nodes** – Besides separating the nodes, we could also implement a mechanism to prevent EU data from leaving Europe. This could be as simple as a view that gives US services access to US data.

A Non-Chinese Company with Chinese Customers

On November 1, 2021, China implemented its first comprehensive data privacy framework, the Personal Information Protection Law (PIPL). Like the CCPA, the PIPL resembles the GDPR, but unlike the GDPR and CCPA, which are focused on individual and consumer rights, respectively, the PIPL is focused on national security.[7]

A company wishing to store the data of Chinese customers must do so within China itself. For us, this means running CockroachDB nodes in China. Any company needing to process Chinese customer data outside of China must undergo a national security review before doing so.[8]

Unless you are a Chinese business, hosting infrastructure in China is not straightforward. An account on AWS will not be sufficient to deploy software to China. You will need to create a separate account on the Chinese AWS site amazonaws.cn by providing Information Security identification and a business registration certificate.

To physically host a site in Mainland China, a company must have a registered Chinese company and complete an ICP (Internet Content Provider) Commercial License.[9]

---

[7]www.wired.co.uk/article/china-personal-data-law

[8]https://digichina.stanford.edu/work/translation-outbound-data-transfer-security-assessment-measures-draft-for-comment-oct-2021/

[9]www.alibabacloud.com/icp

Personally Identifiable Information

Personally Identifiable Information (PII) is a golden ticket to large fines to companies who mishandle it. While the definition of PII may change from country to country, you can think of it as being any personal information that could potentially identify someone. For example, names, addresses, and financial and geographic information could all be used to identify someone.

Here is a nonexhaustive list of PII storage considerations:

- **Payment information** – Your responsibilities to customers will be far greater if you store their financial information, not to mention your compliance requirements. Try to delegate the responsibility of storing payment information to a payment provider if you have one.

- **Names** – Names are perhaps the most obvious way to identify someone. You might need to store a user's name to contact them, process a payment, or make a delivery to them. If your website doesn't need to store their name (or their full name), keep this to a minimum.

- **Contacting customers** – If a user does not permit you to contact them, consider obfuscating their email address, so it's impossible to email them. This could be as simple as hashing their email address, a process that would still allow you to re-hash and verify their email address at login without having it stored in plaintext.

Encryption

With global regulations and PII considered, the next line of defense for data is encryption. Properly implemented, encryption makes it all but impossible for a bad actor to understand and use your data for malicious purposes. In this section, we'll cover data encryption in CockroachDB.

At a high level, there are two areas to focus on when using encryption:

- **Data in transit** – This concerns data travelling between nodes and end users or between nodes.

- **Data at rest** – This concerns data stored on a physical disk. CockroachDB provides two ways of doing this, and I'll introduce you to both.

In Transit

By default, CockroachDB will attempt to start securely and look for certificates and keys to use on startup. If you try to run the following command without generating certificates or keys, CockroachDB will fail to start:

```
$ cockroach start-single-node
*
* ERROR: ERROR: cannot load certificates.
* Check your certificate settings, set --certs-dir, or use --insecure for
insecure clusters.
*
* failed to start server: problem using security settings: no certificates
found; does certs dir exist?
*

...
```

Up to this point, my focus has been to demonstrate runtime CockroachDB features, so I've been using the --insecure flag to bypass this check and run the database insecurely. For anything other than a local installation of CockroachDB for development purposes, you should by securing your cluster with certificates. Let's do that now.

First, create two directories: one to store certificates and one to store keys. Note that once CockroachDB has generated certificates and keys, both of these directories will contain sensitive information:

```
$ mkdir certs
$ mkdir keys
```

Next, we'll ask CockroachDB to generate a Certificate Authority (CA) certificate and a private key. We'll use these files to create certificates for nodes in subsequent steps:

```
$ cockroach cert create-ca \
    --certs-dir=certs \
    --ca-key=keys/ca.key
```

```
$ ls certs
ca.crt

$ ls keys
ca.key
```

Next, we'll ask CockroachDB to generate a certificate and a public/private key pair for the cluster nodes:

```
$ cockroach cert create-node \
    --certs-dir=certs \
    --ca-key=keys/ca.key \
    localhost

$ ls certs
ca.crt   node.crt   node.key

$ ls keys
ca.key
```

The "cert -> create-node" command earlier takes a variadic set of host arguments to aid in node discovery. I'm running everything locally in this example, so passing a single value of "localhost" is sufficient.

Now let's start some CockroachDB nodes using the certificate and key we generated. Previously, CockroachDB returned an error when we attempted to do this, but now we have the files it requires to start securely, so it will start without issue:

```
$ cockroach start \
    --certs-dir=certs \
    --store=node1 \
    --listen-addr=localhost:26257 \
    --http-addr=localhost:8080 \
    --join=localhost:26257,localhost:26258,localhost:26259

$ cockroach start \
    --certs-dir=certs \
    --store=node2 \
    --listen-addr=localhost:26258 \
    --http-addr=localhost:8081 \
    --join=localhost:26257,localhost:26258,localhost:26259
```

```
$ cockroach start \
    --certs-dir=certs \
    --store=node3 \
    --listen-addr=localhost:26259 \
    --http-addr=localhost:8082 \
    --join=localhost:26257,localhost:26258,localhost:26259
```

Let's connect to our cluster. As this is a secure cluster, we'll need to generate and provide a certificate to authenticate users. We'll generate a client certificate for the database root user and use that to connect. First, generate the root client certificate:

```
$ cockroach cert create-client \
    root \
    --certs-dir=certs \
    --ca-key=keys/ca.key
```

We can now initialize the nodes and finish the cluster setup:

```
$ cockroach init --certs-dir=certs --host=localhost:26257
```

Finally, connect to the cluster as the root user using the client certificate we generated:

```
$ cockroach sql --certs-dir=certs
```

If you open a browser to the CockroachDB admin console (https://localhost:8080) now, you'll be asked to log in with a username and password. These will have to be created from the CockroachDB shell as follows:

```
CREATE USER rob WITH PASSWORD 'A_STRONG_PASSWORD';
```

The CockroachDB admin console requires logged-in users to have admin permissions to see certain elements (e.g., Node Map). Let's give this user admin privileges ahead of time:

```
GRANT ADMIN TO rob WITH ADMIN OPTION;
```

At Rest

Encryption at rest is an Enterprise feature of CockroachDB. It will encrypt data on-disk transparently, meaning a user with proper access to the data will never be aware that encryption took place.

CockroachDB uses the Advanced Encryption Standard (AES) algorithm to encrypt data with a key size of either 128, 192, or 256 bits.

To generate an encryption key, simply invoke the gen command of the cockroach binary. The following command generates a 256 AES key that we'll use for the rest of this chapter:

```
$ cockroach gen encryption-key -s 256 keys/enc.key
```

You must manage this key securely. If it gets into the wrong hands, your data will be available to anyone with access to your CockroachDB nodes. Cockroach Labs has the following recommendations for managing encryption keys:

- Only the UNIX user running the CockroachDB process should have access to encryption keys.

- You should not store encryption keys in the same place as your CockroachDB data. Something like HashiCorp's Vault would be a good candidate for this.

- Rotate encryption keys regularly. Every few weeks to months.

Database Encryption

Database encryption involves encrypting all of the tables within a database. If you are unsure whether specific tables need encrypting or not, this is a sensible option, as it ensures everything is encrypted.

First, let's create some nodes. With one difference, these commands are similar to the commands we used to start the nodes in the encryption in-transit section. In the following commands, we provide an additional --enterprise-encryption argument that tells CockroachDB that we'll be using Enterprise encryption features.

The --enterprise-encryption argument uses key-value pairs to configure encryption-specific configurations:

- **path** – The directory that will store your CockroachDB data. This value corresponds to the value provided to the --store argument.

- **key** – The absolute or relative path to the current encryption key.

- **old-key** – The absolute or relative path to the previous encryption key. Use "plain" to tell CockroachDB to fall back to storing data in plaintext (a.k.a. unencrypted).

- **rotation-period** – The period after which CockroachDB will automatically rotate your encryption keys.

The following commands create three nodes with encryption enabled. For consistency, I will reuse the certificates generated in the previous section:

```
$ cockroach start \
    --certs-dir=certs \
    --store=node1 \
    --listen-addr=localhost:26257 \
    --http-addr=localhost:8080 \
    --join=localhost:26257,localhost:26258,localhost:26259 \
    --enterprise-encryption=path=node1,key=keys/enc.key,old-key=plain

$ cockroach start \
    --certs-dir=certs \
    --store=node2 \
    --listen-addr=localhost:26258 \
    --http-addr=localhost:8081 \
    --join=localhost:26257,localhost:26258,localhost:26259 \
    --enterprise-encryption=path=node2,key=keys/enc.key,old-key=plain

$ cockroach start \
    --certs-dir=certs \
    --store=node3 \
    --listen-addr=localhost:26259 \
    --http-addr=localhost:8082 \
    --join=localhost:26257,localhost:26258,localhost:26259 \
    --enterprise-encryption=path=node3,key=keys/enc.key,old-key=plain
```

Now, initialize the cluster with the following command:

```
$ cockroach init --certs-dir=certs --host=localhost:26257
```

If you open the CockroachDB admin console and navigate to the following URLs, you'll see that each of the nodes has one encrypted data store, encrypted with the key we generated, as is shown in Figure 6-1:

- **Node 1** – `https://localhost:8080/#/reports/stores/1`

- **Node 2** – `https://localhost:8080/#/reports/stores/2`

- **Node 3** – `https://localhost:8080/#/reports/stores/3`

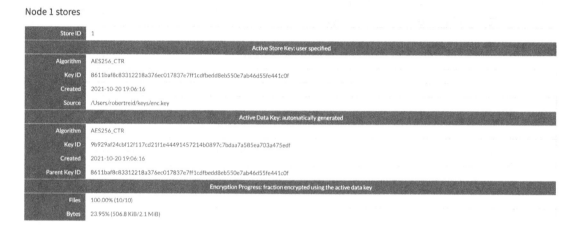

Stores

Node 1 stores

Store ID	1
Active Store Key: user specified	
Algorithm	AES256_CTR
Key ID	8611baf8c83312218a376ec017837e7ff1cdfbedd8eb550e7ab46d55fe441c0f
Created	2021-10-20 19:06:16
Source	/Users/robertreid/keys/enc.key
Active Data Key: automatically generated	
Algorithm	AES256_CTR
Key ID	9b929af24cbf12f117cd21f1e44491457214b0897c7bdaa7a585ea703a475edf
Created	2021-10-20 19:06:16
Parent Key ID	8611baf8c83312218a376ec017837e7ff1cdfbedd8eb550e7ab46d55fe441c0f
Encryption Progress: fraction encrypted using the active data key	
Files	100.00% (10/10)
Bytes	23.95% (506.8 KiB/2.1 MiB)

Figure 6-1. *The Node 1 data stores view*

Table Encryption

CockroachDB also allows you to encrypt specific tables rather than encrypting an entire cluster. For example, suppose your database has some huge tables that don't contain sensitive information. In that case, this might be a good option for you, as you won't pay the performance penalty of decrypting encrypted data.

Creating a cluster that supports table encryption is similar to creating an encrypted cluster. However, there are two small changes you need to make to the startup commands:

- **`--store`** – This argument now provides a set of key/value pairs rather than a simple string, which tells CockroachDB where to store your encrypted and unencrypted data. In the following example, I'm telling CockroachDB to encrypt the "node1/encrypted" directory and not encrypt the "node1/unencrypted" directory.

- **`--enterprise-encryption`** – This argument needs to be updated to point at just the encrypted data directory.

The following commands create three nodes with partial encryption enabled. I will continue securing my cluster for consistency:

```
$ cockroach start \
    --certs-dir=certs \
    --store=path=node1/encrypted,attrs=encrypted \
    --store=path=node1/unencrypted,attrs=unencrypted \
    --listen-addr=localhost:26257 \
    --http-addr=localhost:8080 \
    --join=localhost:26257,localhost:26258,localhost:26259 \
    --enterprise-encryption=path=node1/encrypted,key=keys/enc.key,old-
key=plain

$ cockroach start \
    --certs-dir=certs \
    --store=path=node2/encrypted,attrs=encrypted \
    --store=path=node2/unencrypted,attrs=unencrypted \
    --listen-addr=localhost:26258 \
    --http-addr=localhost:8081 \
    --join=localhost:26257,localhost:26258,localhost:26259 \
    --enterprise-encryption=path=node2/encrypted,key=keys/enc.key,old-
key=plain

$ cockroach start \
    --certs-dir=certs \
    --store=path=node3/encrypted,attrs=encrypted \
    --store=path=node3/unencrypted,attrs=unencrypted \
    --listen-addr=localhost:26259 \
    --http-addr=localhost:8082 \
    --join=localhost:26257,localhost:26258,localhost:26259 \
    --enterprise-encryption=path=node3/encrypted,key=keys/enc.key,old-
key=plain
```

Now, initialize the cluster with the following command:

```
$ cockroach init --certs-dir=certs --host=localhost:26257
```

With the cluster initialized, we can now connect to it using the root user client certificate we created previously:

```
$ cockroach sql --certs-dir=certs
```

It's time to create some encrypted and unencrypted tables. We do this by first identifying the tables we need to and don't need to encrypt. In the following example, I'm creating a customer table containing Personally Identifiable Information (PII), which should be encrypted, and a product table containing no PII, which does not need to be encrypted.

Let's create the customer and product tables now:

```
CREATE TABLE customer (
    id UUID PRIMARY KEY DEFAULT gen_random_uuid(),
    first_name string NOT NULL,
    last_name string NOT NULL
);
ALTER TABLE customer CONFIGURE ZONE USING CONSTRAINTS = '[+encrypted]';

CREATE TABLE product (
    id UUID PRIMARY KEY DEFAULT gen_random_uuid(),
    name string NOT NULL
);
ALTER TABLE product CONFIGURE ZONE USING CONSTRAINTS = '[+unencrypted]';
```

After creating each table in the example shown previously, I'm setting zone configurations to mark a table as being either +encrypted (needs encrypting) or +unencrypted (does not need encrypting). These constraints coincide with the attributes we used when defining the stores earlier.

If you open the CockroachDB admin console and navigate to the data source URLs again, you'll see that each of the nodes has an encrypted store and an unencrypted store, as is shown in Figure 6-2.

Stores

Node 1 stores

Store ID	1
Active Store Key: user specified	
Algorithm	AES256_CTR
Key ID	8611baf8c83312218a376ec017837e7ff1cdfbedd8eb550e7ab46d55fe441c0f
Created	2021-10-20 19:24:57
Source	/Users/robertreid/keys/enc.key
Active Data Key: automatically generated	
Algorithm	AES256_CTR
Key ID	a8a27d2584f337e95d4259f1c3669c2666e1376991ca67a27169dfe0e78194af
Created	2021-10-20 19:24:25
Parent Key ID	8611baf8c83312218a376ec017837e7ff1cdfbedd8eb550e7ab46d55fe441c0f
Encryption Progress: fraction encrypted using the active data key	
Files	100.00% (9/9)
Bytes	26.29% (103.0 KiB/391.7 KiB)

Store ID	2
Encryption status	Not encrypted

Figure 6-2. *The Node 1 data stores*

CHAPTER 7

Deployment Topologies

In this chapter, we'll explore some common cluster deployment topologies. Each will make sense in different circumstances, depending on your environment, latency, and survivability requirements.

I'll create an example cluster for many of the topologies listed in this chapter to show you how it's done. To balance clarity with succinctness, I will manually create CockroachDB nodes for all of the examples in this chapter. Depending on your infrastructure and preferred deployment and orchestration technologies, you may prefer to deploy with Kubernetes or use Cockroach Cloud. Note also that in this chapter, I aim to show just the relationships between nodes. I won't be deploying geographically separate nodes.

I'll reuse some generated certificates and keys for all clusters to reduce repetition. I'll create these with the following commands:

```
$ mkdir certs
$ mkdir keys

$ cockroach cert create-ca \
    --certs-dir=certs \
    --ca-key=keys/ca.key

$ cockroach cert create-node \
    --certs-dir=certs \
    --ca-key=keys/ca.key \
    localhost

$ cockroach cert create-client \
    root \
    --certs-dir=certs \
    --ca-key=keys/ca.key
```

© Rob Reid 2022
R. Reid, *Practical CockroachDB*, https://doi.org/10.1007/978-1-4842-8224-3_7

Single-Region Topologies

We'll start with the single-region topologies. These are recommended for small-scale clusters that serve users from a single location. For example, these topologies will work for you if you're a UK business with only UK customers. Let's explore them.

Development

You'll likely want to keep costs to a minimum during the course of development. For this reason, Cockroach Labs acknowledges that a single-node cluster works well for this scenario, if you are prepared to prioritize cost-savings and simplicity over resiliency. The Development Topology defines exactly this: a CockroachDB cluster with a single node.

I would give a single-node cluster the following characteristics:

Read latency	★★★★★	The gateway node is also the leaseholder node for all data, meaning no internode hops required.
Write latency	★★★★★	No replication latencies incurred.
Resiliency	★	A single-node cluster offers no protection against machine or network failures.
Ease of setup	★★★★★	Can be installed onto a machine on the local network or an E2C server, etc.

A development cluster like this will exhibit different performance characteristics to a distributed cluster. Care should be taken to thoroughly test an accurate representation of your production cluster before real users start interacting with your application.

Basic Production

Once your application has users who depend on an available database, a single-node cluster is no longer a viable topology. The Basic Production topology defines a CockroachDB cluster with nodes in multiple availability zones (AZs) in a single region.

The number of nodes you choose to deploy is up to you, but in order to survive an outage of a single AZ, you'll need at least three nodes with a replication factor of three. In order to survive an outage of two AZs, you'll need at least five nodes with a replication factor of five.

The architecture of a Basic Production topology will typically resemble Figure 7-1.

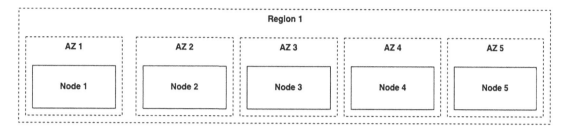

Figure 7-1. *Architecture of a cluster using the Basic Production topology*

Let's look at some of the benefits and drawbacks of a cluster using this topology:

Read latency	★★★★★	The gateway node is in the same region as the leaseholder nodes.
Write latency	★★★★★	All replication occurs within the same region, so consensus is achieved quickly.
Resiliency	★★★	Can survive single/multiple AZ outages depending on your architecture, node count, and replication strategy.
Ease of setup	★★★★	All nodes exist within a single region, so they can be easily orchestrated with Kubernetes with little effort.

Now, let's create a cluster to simulate the Basic Production topology. Let's create a five-node cluster that can handle an outage of two AZs:

```
$ cockroach start \
    --certs-dir=certs \
    --store=node1 \
    --listen-addr=localhost:26257 \
    --http-addr=localhost:8080 \
    --locality=region=us-east1,zone=a \
    --join=localhost:26257,localhost:26258,localhost:26259,localhost:26260,
      localhost:262561

$ cockroach start \
    --certs-dir=certs \
    --store=node2 \
    --listen-addr=localhost:26258 \
```

```
    --http-addr=localhost:8081 \
    --locality=region=us-east1,zone=b \
    --join=localhost:26257,localhost:26258,localhost:26259,localhost:26260,
      localhost:262561

$ cockroach start \
    --certs-dir=certs \
    --store=node3 \
    --listen-addr=localhost:26259 \
    --http-addr=localhost:8082 \
    --locality=region=us-east1,zone=c \
    --join=localhost:26257,localhost:26258,localhost:26259,localhost:26260,
      localhost:262561

$ cockroach start \
    --certs-dir=certs \
    --store=node4 \
    --listen-addr=localhost:26260 \
    --http-addr=localhost:8083 \
    --locality=region=us-east1,zone=d \
    --join=localhost:26257,localhost:26258,localhost:26259,localhost:26260,
      localhost:262561

$ cockroach start \
    --certs-dir=certs \
    --store=node5 \
    --listen-addr=localhost:26261 \
    --http-addr=localhost:8084 \
    --locality=region=us-east1,zone=e \
    --join=localhost:26257,localhost:26258,localhost:26259,localhost:26260,
      localhost:262561

$ cockroach init --certs-dir=certs --host=localhost:26257
```

Next, we'll connect to the cluster and run some commands to ensure CockroachDB replicates our data across the five nodes.

```
$ cockroach sql --certs-dir=certs

ALTER RANGE default CONFIGURE ZONE USING num_replicas = 5;

CREATE TABLE example();

SELECT lease_holder_locality, replicas
FROM [SHOW RANGES FROM TABLE example];
  lease_holder_locality  |  replicas
-------------------------+--------------
  region=us-east1,zone=e | {1,2,3,4,5}
```

The increase in replicas from three to five can take a minute or two to take effect, but once it has, you'll notice that CockroachDB uses all five of the nodes as replicas for data in the example table. If we lose two of the five nodes, the remaining three will still manage to achieve quorum.

Multiregion Topologies

Multiregion topologies are good for applications requiring a higher degree of failure tolerance. I'd recommend these topologies for clusters that need to span larger geographic areas, with customers in multiple locations. I'd also recommend these topologies if your survival goals include the outage of an entire cloud region, regardless of where your customers are situated. For example, if you're an EU-based business with customers in Europe and Asia, these topologies will work well. Let's explore them.

Regional Tables

The Regional Tables topology is a good choice for scenarios where you need to pin data to specific regions. In this configuration, you'll ensure that data for users in a given region is always close to them, making for fast local region reads and writes.

As multiregion clusters span not just AZs but whole regions, the number of nodes will typically be higher. For a cluster capable of surviving not just AZ but also region failures, the node count will jump from a minimum of between three and five nodes to between nine and fifteen. Figure 7-2 shows a multiregion cluster capable of surviving regional outages but not AZ outages. In an AZ outage, customers closest to the now unavailable *region* will route to another region, increasing latency.

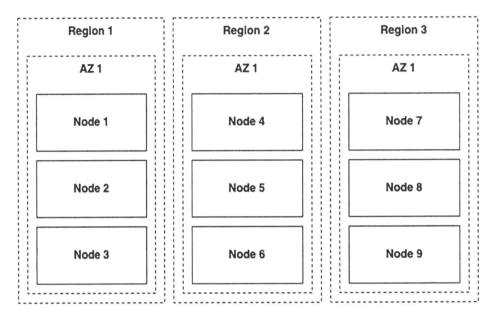

Figure 7-2. *Architecture of a cluster using the Regional Tables topology*

Let's look at some of the benefits and drawbacks of a cluster using this topology:

Read latency	★★★★	If data is pinned to a single region, reads from that region will be quick. If data is not pinned and comes from multiple regions, you'll incur interregion latency.
Write latency	★★★★	If data is pinned to a single region, writes to that region will be quick. If data is replicated across regions (for higher resiliency), you'll incur interregion replication latency.
Resiliency	★★★★	If you replicate data across regions, you'll achieve resilience against regional failures. If you pin data to regions and have nodes in different AZs within that region, you'll achieve resilience against AZ failure.
Ease of setup	★★★	Setting up a multiregion cluster is not without its pains. If you're orchestrating your cluster in Kubernetes, you'll need a cluster for each region, and their networks will need to be peered.

Now let's create a cluster to simulate the Regional Tables topology. In this example, we'll create a nine-node cluster that's capable of surviving regional outages. We'll reuse the start commands from the "Multiregion Clusters" section in Chapter 2 to save repetition.

Next, we'll set up our database and regions (note that an Enterprise license is required for geo-partitioning):

```
CREATE DATABASE topologies_demo;
USE topologies_demo;

ALTER DATABASE "topologies_demo" PRIMARY REGION "us-east1";
ALTER DATABASE "topologies_demo" ADD REGION "us-central1";
ALTER DATABASE "topologies_demo" ADD REGION "us-west1";

ALTER DATABASE "topologies_demo" SURVIVE REGION FAILURE;
```

With the cluster up and running, let's create two tables: one that's completely regional (i.e., all data remains in one region) and another whose rows will be pinned to different regions. First, we'll create the regional table and insert a single row into it:

```
CREATE TABLE example_regional_table(
  id UUID PRIMARY KEY DEFAULT gen_random_uuid()
);
ALTER TABLE example_regional_table SET LOCALITY REGIONAL BY TABLE IN
"us-central1";

INSERT INTO example_regional_table DEFAULT VALUES;
```

Next, we'll create the table that's regional by row and insert three rows into it, one for each region:

```
CREATE TABLE example_regional_rows (
    id UUID PRIMARY KEY DEFAULT gen_random_uuid(),
    city TEXT NOT NULL,
    crdb_region crdb_internal_region NOT NULL AS (
      CASE
      WHEN city IN ('Charleston', 'Columbia', 'North Charleston') THEN
      'us-east1'
```

```
        WHEN city IN ('Des Moines', 'Cedar Rapids', 'Davenport') THEN
          'us-central1'
        WHEN city IN ('Portland', 'Eugene', 'Salem') THEN 'us-west1'
        ELSE 'us-central1'
          END
        ) STORED
);

ALTER TABLE example_regional_rows SET LOCALITY REGIONAL BY ROW;

INSERT into example_regional_rows (city)
VALUES
        ('Charleston'),
        ('Des Moines'),
        ('Portland');
```

Give CockroachDB a minute or so to allow replication to finish and inspect the ranges. The following statements are formatted to make them easier to read:

```
SELECT lease_holder_locality, replicas, replica_localities
FROM [SHOW RANGES FROM TABLE example_regional_table];

region=us-central1,zone=us-central1b
{1,2,4,6,8}
{
    "region=us-east1,zone=us-east1a",
    "region=us-east1,zone=us-east1b",
    "region=us-central1,zone=us-central1c",
    "region=us-central1,zone=us-central1b",
    "region=us-west1,zone=us-west1b"
}

SELECT lease_holder_locality, replicas, replica_localities
FROM [SHOW RANGES FROM TABLE example_regional_rows]
WHERE "start_key" NOT LIKE '%Prefix%';
```

```
region=us-central1,zone=us-central1b
{1,3,4,6,8}
{
    "region=us-east1,zone=us-east1a",
    "region=us-east1,zone=us-east1c",
    "region=us-central1,zone=us-central1c",
    "region=us-central1,zone=us-central1b",
    "region=us-west1,zone=us-west1b"
}

region=us-east1,zone=us-east1a
{1,3,5,7,8}
{
    "region=us-east1,zone=us-east1a",
    "region=us-east1,zone=us-east1c",
    "region=us-central1,zone=us-central1a",
    "region=us-west1,zone=us-west1a",
    "region=us-west1,zone=us-west1b"
}

region=us-west1,zone=us-west1b
{1,4,6,7,8}
{
    "region=us-east1,zone=us-east1a",
    "region=us-central1,zone=us-central1c",
    "region=us-central1,zone=us-central1b",
    "region=us-west1,zone=us-west1a",
    "region=us-west1,zone=us-west1b"
}
```

The default replication factor is five, so you can see that nodes from all regions have been used to store the data. This is because CockroachDB does not know why you're geo-partitioning data, so it tries to replicate data in as resilient a way as possible, given the default survival goal of REGION. This is acceptable when data can flow freely between regions, but not acceptable when it needs to be pinned for regulatory reasons.

Note that the example_regional_table has two nodes within us-central1, and its leaseholder is also in us-central1.

Note that in the example_regional_rows table (a table whose *rows* are region specific), there are two nodes for each of the geo-partitioned regions used by the tables. Like the example_regional_table example, the range leaseholder also exists within that region.

If you require data to exist in a single region, you'll need to change the survival goal of the database from REGION to ZONE and update the replicator factor to reflect the number of nodes in that region. This cluster has three regions and three nodes in each of those regions, so the commands to reflect this are

```
ALTER DATABASE "topologies_demo" SURVIVE ZONE FAILURE;

SET override_multi_region_zone_config = true;
ALTER TABLE example_regional_rows CONFIGURE ZONE USING num_voters = 3;
ALTER TABLE example_regional_rows CONFIGURE ZONE USING num_replicas = 3;

SET override_multi_region_zone_config = true;
ALTER TABLE example_regional_table CONFIGURE ZONE USING num_voters = 3;
ALTER TABLE example_regional_table CONFIGURE ZONE USING num_replicas = 3;
```

After a minute or so, check table ranges again. This time, you'll notice that because we've explicitly removed our requirement to survive regional failures, all data now exists in the region we configured for the tables:

```
SELECT lease_holder_locality, replicas, replica_localities
FROM [SHOW RANGES FROM TABLE example_regional_table];

region=us-central1,zone=us-central1a
{4,6,9}
{
    "region=us-central1,zone=us-central1c",
    "region=us-central1,zone=us-central1a",
    "region=us-central1,zone=us-central1b"
}

SELECT lease_holder_locality, replicas, replica_localities
FROM [SHOW RANGES FROM TABLE example_regional_rows]
WHERE "start_key" NOT LIKE '%Prefix%';
```

```
region=us-central1,zone=us-central1c
{4,6,9}
{
    "region=us-central1,zone=us-central1c",
    "region=us-central1,zone=us-central1a",
    "region=us-central1,zone=us-central1b"
}

region=us-east1,zone=us-east1a
{1,2,3}
{
    "region=us-east1,zone=us-east1a",
    "region=us-east1,zone=us-east1b",
    "region=us-east1,zone=us-east1c"
}

region=us-west1,zone=us-west1b
{5,7,8}
{
    "region=us-west1,zone=us-west1b",
    "region=us-west1,zone=us-west1a",
    "region=us-west1,zone=us-west1c"
}
```

Global Tables

The Global Tables topology is a good choice for read-heavy scenarios where write latencies can be tolerated. Reads will be managed locally to a region and therefore fast, whereas writes will replicate across regions, so they will be much slower.

Let's look at some of the benefits and drawbacks of a cluster using this topology:

Read latency	★★★★	If data is pinned to a single region, reads from that region will be quick. If data is not pinned and comes from multiple regions, you'll incur interregion latency.
Write latency	★★	Data is replicated across regions before write statements return.
Resiliency	★★★★★	If you replicate data across regions, you'll achieve resilience against regional failures. If you pin data to regions and have nodes in different AZs within that region, you'll achieve resilience against AZ failure.
Ease of setup	★★★	Setting up a Global Tables cluster is similar to setting up a Region Tables cluster.

To enable the Global Tables topology pattern, we simply need to update the configuration of a table to make it global. For this example, I'll update our example_regional_table to be global:

```
ALTER TABLE example_regional_table SET LOCALITY GLOBAL;
```

You may notice that the replication count has gone from three to five. This is the default replication count for global tables, and it allows CockroachDB to scale the table beyond the existing us-central1 region:

```
SELECT lease_holder_locality, replicas, replica_localities
FROM [SHOW RANGES FROM TABLE example_regional_table];

region=us-east1,zone=us-east1a
{1,2,3,5,9}
{
    "region=us-east1,zone=us-east1a",
    "region=us-east1,zone=us-east1b",
    "region=us-east1,zone=us-east1c",
    "region=us-west1,zone=us-west1b",
    "region=us-central1,zone=us-central1b"
}
```

Follower Reads

The Follower Reads topology is a good choice for read-heavy scenarios where reads for stale data and write latencies can be tolerated. The stale tolerance afforded by this pattern reduces read and write contention for the same data, as the data can be requested for slightly different time periods. The level of read staleness will depend on your requirements and can be one of the following:

- **Exact Staleness** – The amount of data staleness is an exact amount (at least 4.8 seconds), so reads are quicker than Bounded Staleness reads.

- **Bounded Staleness** – CockroachDB determines the amount of data staleness dynamically, minimizing staleness. Availability is higher than Exact Staleness because reads can be served from local replicas rather than leaseholders in the event of a network partition.

Let's look at some of the benefits and drawbacks of a cluster using this topology:

Read latency	★★★★★	Reads are very fast because latency is prioritized over consistency.
Write latency	★★	Data is replicated across regions before write statements return.
Resiliency	★★★★★	The cluster can tolerate failures of AZs and regions.
Ease of setup	★★★	The configuration for Follower Reads is provided by clients during reads, so this topology is no more difficult than any other multiregion cluster.

To enable the Follower Reads topology, we simply need to make SELECT queries that allow for staleness. The following query is a follower-read query against the example_regional_rows table:

```
SELECT * FROM example_regional_rows
  AS OF SYSTEM TIME follower_read_timestamp();

              id                   |    city    | crdb_region
-----------------------------------+------------+--------------
 7b65d3fa-a0e1-4cd6-b125-05654a6fbce8 | Portland   | us-west1
 d39ec728-cfc0-47e8-914c-fff493064071 | Des Moines | us-central1
 e6a0c79c-2026-4877-b24f-6d4d9dd86848 | Charleston | us-east1
```

It's also possible to enable follower reads within transactions using the following syntax:

```
BEGIN;
SET TRANSACTION AS OF SYSTEM TIME follower_read_timestamp();
SELECT * FROM example_regional_rows;
COMMIT;
```

Using the `follower_read_timestamp()` function is not only convenient but returns a timestamp that increases the likelihood of your query returning data from the local region.

Follow-the-Workload

The Follow-the-Workload topology is the default topology for clusters that do not specify a table locality (e.g., regional by rows). They are a good choice for scenarios where read latencies in the current most active region must be low.

In a cluster using the Follow-the-Workload topology, CockroachDB will move data to ensure that the busiest region for reads gets the required data.

Let's look at some of the benefits and drawbacks of a cluster using this topology:

Read latency	★★★★	Reads for data within the current busiest region will be fast, whereas reads from outside that region will be slower.
Write latency	★★	Data is replicated across regions before write statements return.
Resiliency	★★★★★	The cluster can tolerate failures of AZs and regions.
Ease of setup	★★★	This topology is the default topology for multiregion clusters, so no more difficult than any other multiregion cluster.

Being the default topology, there's nothing we need to do to explicitly enable it.

Antipatterns

Considering antipatterns and the performance implications of a poorly designed cluster is as critical as considering the recommended topology patterns. In this section, we'll create a cluster using the demo command that *seems* well designed but will have poor performance characteristics.

First, we'll spin up the cluster. This cluster will be a nine-node, multiregion deployment, with nodes in us-west1, us-east1, and europe-west1.

```
$ cockroach demo --nodes 9 --no-example-database
```

Next, we'll create some database objects. The following statements will

- Create a database called antipatterns_database with three regions, reflecting the regions created by the demo command

- Create a regional table whose rows will be geographically distributed between the regions

- Insert data for each of the regions

- Update the table's zone configuration to ensure that data stays within those regions

```
CREATE DATABASE antipattern_database;
USE antipattern_database;

ALTER DATABASE "antipattern_database" PRIMARY REGION "us-east1";
ALTER DATABASE "antipattern_database" ADD REGION "us-west1";
ALTER DATABASE "antipattern_database" ADD REGION "europe-west1";

ALTER DATABASE "antipattern_database" SURVIVE ZONE FAILURE;

CREATE TABLE antipattern_table (
    id UUID PRIMARY KEY DEFAULT gen_random_uuid(),
    city TEXT NOT NULL,
    crdb_region crdb_internal_region NOT NULL AS (
      CASE
    WHEN city IN ('New York', 'Boston', 'Chicago') THEN 'us-east1'
    WHEN city IN ('San Francisco', 'Portland', 'Seattle') THEN 'us-west1'
    WHEN city IN ('Berlin', 'Paris', 'Madrid') THEN 'europe-west1'
    ELSE 'europe-west1'
      END
    ) STORED
);
```

```
ALTER TABLE antipattern_table SET LOCALITY REGIONAL BY ROW;

INSERT into antipattern_table (city)
VALUES
      ('New York'), ('Boston'), ('Chicago'),
      ('San Francisco'), ('Portland'), ('Seattle'),
      ('Berlin'), ('Paris'), ('Madrid');

SET override_multi_region_zone_config = true;
ALTER TABLE antipattern_table CONFIGURE ZONE USING num_voters = 3;
ALTER TABLE antipattern_table CONFIGURE ZONE USING num_replicas = 3;
```

What we've essentially created with these commands is a globally distributed follow-the-workload cluster. If the most active region is Europe in this example, queries against the antipattern_table will have to fetch data from the States and vice versa.

After a short while, run the following statement to ensure that data has been distributed equally between the nodes:

```
SELECT lease_holder_locality, replicas, replica_localities
FROM [SHOW RANGES FROM TABLE antipattern_table]
WHERE "start_key" NOT LIKE '%Prefix%';

region=europe-west1,az=c
{7,8,9}
{
    "region=europe-west1,az=b",
    "region=europe-west1,az=c",
    "region=europe-west1,az=d"
}

region=us-east1,az=d
{1,2,3}
{
    "region=us-east1,az=b",
    "region=us-east1,az=c",
    "region=us-east1,az=d"
}
```

```
region=us-west1,az=b
{4,5,6}
{
    "region=us-west1,az=a",
    "region=us-west1,az=b",
    "region=us-west1,az=c"
}
```

Now let's perform a query to check the latency:

```
SELECT * FROM antipattern_table;
```

```
                 id                  |     city      | crdb_region
-------------------------------------+---------------+---------------
  3c24dee9-f006-4c2a-b556-0d7d6d0a7f6d | Portland      | us-west1
  8aaab90d-2ff3-471b-ac5a-39eec13b97bd | San Francisco | us-west1
  9489216e-95f2-4796-98bd-ba654f85b688 | Seattle       | us-west1
  421f2184-99d7-4d2a-823c-e330ccbf5a87 | Madrid        | europe-west1
  48b68338-93b2-4761-832b-4a3a91ba77e5 | Berlin        | europe-west1
  731b6876-d745-47f3-822e-d2fe2867d639 | Paris         | europe-west1
  a1542138-f0ff-41ba-bfa7-1da3a5226103 | New York      | us-east1
  c66acd43-e23f-47ce-9965-6b09d6c4e502 | Chicago       | us-east1
  c73e23a1-65c1-4063-8f93-51094e0fe475 | Boston        | us-east1
(9 rows)
```

```
Time: 14ms total (execution 14ms / network 0ms)
```

If you thought that 14ms for CockroachDB to gather data from the east and west coast of the States and west Europe was impressive, you'd be right! Unfortunately, this highlights an important oversight in the configuration of this database. Running the demo command by itself does not simulate interregion latencies. We need to add the --global flag to enable this.

This time, we'll run the demo command as follows:

```
$ cockroach demo --global --nodes 9 --no-example-database
```

If you run the same SQL commands against the database this time, you see different results, once the data has replicated into the configured regions:

```
SELECT * FROM antipattern_table;
                   id                   |     city      |  crdb_region
----------------------------------------+---------------+---------------
  8c9600f7-81b2-40df-8d3c-9e00404bce7f  | Paris         | europe-west1
  8d21288b-12f7-438d-8ef1-d51e7d3335be  | Madrid        | europe-west1
  de45d851-f25b-4c4b-90aa-4193c469c82c  | Berlin        | europe-west1
  0c04c9dd-4752-4489-a71f-3f13edae8923  | Boston        | us-east1
  87f4043b-d611-4129-a50e-dc941788110f  | Chicago       | us-east1
  d6ed2ab1-93d4-4306-8ef7-ec2bc00027f8  | New York      | us-east1
  948d90e2-e382-4e82-92fc-a57679ebf577  | Seattle       | us-west1
  bc21e9e4-5929-47fa-a2e9-b7ff7cc29bec  | San Francisco | us-west1
  c41f5a0c-f854-4815-ac3d-62eb3efe4147  | Portland      | us-west1
(9 rows)

Time: 929ms total (execution 928ms / network 0ms)
```

Subsequent queries will perform faster because of caching, but the design of our cluster topology is not currently optimal. There are various ways this can be improved upon:

- **Views** – If some of your users require access to real-time global data, you could consider placing some geographically sensitive data behind views and have regional users connect to their local cluster with a region-specific database user. The view would expose just the data that's closest to the user, meaning no globally distributed queries. We did just this in the "Restrict Table Data" section in Chapter 5.

- **Separate clusters** – If you need compliant, global reach but not necessarily global data (e.g., one, globally queryable database), you could create separate clusters that only span regions that are close to one another (e.g., us-west1, us-central1, and us-east1). This way, you'll achieve data privacy compliance and regional resilience. If you need access to all of global data but don't necessarily need it in real time, you could configure CDC to update the data in a centralized store asynchronously. Just as we did in the "Watching for Database Changes" section in Chapter 5.

Summary

You'll need to carefully design your production cluster to get the best out of it. The following points will help you cover the fundamentals:

- **Read latencies** – Read latencies are good across the majority of topologies. When designing your cluster, consider the implications of pinning data to specific regions if you're not locking data into those regions with something like views. A query for all data in a geo-partitioned database will result in cross-regional reads and increased latencies.

- **Write latencies** – Write latencies between topologies vary to a greater degree than read latencies. There are latency implications to consider when using cross-region replication. If you require regional resilience, consider replicating to a set of local regions (e.g., replicating europe-west1 data to europe-north1 and europe-central1, for example, rather than to australia-southeast2 and us-west1).

- **Testing** – The best way to test your cluster and any applied topology patterns is to spin up a real-world cluster and monitor its performance. If this is not possible, you can simulate globally distributed clusters with the `--demo` command or by using Docker and the HAProxy container.[1]

---

[1] `www.cockroachlabs.com/blog/simulate-cockroachdb-cluster-localhost-docker`

CHAPTER 8

Testing

In this chapter, we'll explore some techniques for testing your database, whether it's on your machine, in your CI/CD pipeline, ready for production, or already in production.

It's easy to overlook the database during application testing. The test areas to neglect during development time are numerous. I'll share a real-world example with you to highlight the importance of having a test strategy when a database is involved.

While developing my first database-backed application, I created a dataset with all row combinations I thought my application would need to support. Whenever I learned of a new requirement, I updated the dataset, and everything seemed to work as expected. Right up to the point where I deployed to production and saw production amounts of data. My application was sluggish and grew increasingly sluggish over the days that followed its deployment.

In this example, I'd neglected to test one significant thing in my database: indexes. With my small (but seemingly comprehensive) dataset, I'd developed a false sense of confidence that my application and database were ready for production. The moment it saw production amounts of data, the missing index reared its ugly head, and my application grew steadily slower.

There are many things you'll want to get your application and database ready for before they come anywhere near your users. There are three high-level types of database tests you'll want to consider to ensure comprehensive test coverage:

- **Structural testing** – Focuses on everything that makes up your database, its schemas, tables, columns, and views.

- **Functional testing** – Focuses on the functionality of your databases. In this stage of testing, you'll ask questions like "how do CRUD operations against its tables affect the resulting state of data?"

- **Nonfunctional testing** – Focuses on everything else (performance and security, etc.).

© Rob Reid 2022

R. Reid, *Practical CockroachDB*, https://doi.org/10.1007/978-1-4842-8224-3_8

Before we get onto testing, let's create a basic (and very contrived) database and work through some testing scenarios together to assert its correctness. First, we'll create a local cluster to more or less mirror a three-node Basic Production topology cluster:

```
$ mkdir certs
$ mkdir keys

$ cockroach cert create-ca \
    --certs-dir=certs \
    --ca-key=keys/ca.key

$ cockroach cert create-node \
    --certs-dir=certs \
    --ca-key=keys/ca.key \
    localhost

$ cockroach start \
    --certs-dir=certs \
    --store=node1 \
    --listen-addr=localhost:26257 \
    --http-addr=localhost:8080 \
    --locality=region=us-east1,zone=a \
    --join=localhost:26257,localhost:26258,localhost:26259

$ cockroach start \
    --certs-dir=certs \
    --store=node2 \
    --listen-addr=localhost:26258 \
    --http-addr=localhost:8081 \
    --locality=region=us-east1,zone=b \
    --join=localhost:26257,localhost:26258,localhost:26259

$ cockroach start \
    --certs-dir=certs \
    --store=node3 \
    --listen-addr=localhost:26259 \
    --http-addr=localhost:8082 \
    --locality=region=us-east1,zone=c \
    --join=localhost:26257,localhost:26258,localhost:26259
```

```
$ cockroach init \
    --certs-dir=certs \
    --host=localhost:26257

$ cockroach cert create-client \
    root \
    --certs-dir=certs \
    --ca-key=keys/ca.key
```

Structural Testing

One of the goals of structural testing is to assert whether the proposed structure of the database and its objects will satisfy business requirements. So rather than creating a bunch of tables up front, I'll go object by object and detail my design decisions for each database object. Remember that this business scenario (and all database objects) is contrived and not production-ready; the resulting database will be bare-bones.

Let's start by creating the database. The company is called Bean About Town (totally fictional, although a quick Google reveals that at least *three* cunning London-based companies have had the same idea). For the commands that follow, we'll use the root user. Let's open a CockroachDB shell and create the database bean_about_town. We will arrange all of our database objects under that:

```
$ cockroach sql \
    --certs-dir=certs

CREATE DATABASE bean_about_town;
USE bean_about_town;
```

There are to be three primary user groups for the database: customers, members of the coffee roasting department, and members of the accounting department. Let's create three users with simple passwords to ensure sensible isolation of grants and privileges. We'll have a retail user with access to customer-facing tables, a roasting user with access to roasting-related tables, and a finance user with access to accounts-related tables:

```
CREATE USER retail_user WITH LOGIN PASSWORD '7efd7222dfdfb107';
CREATE USER roasting_user WITH LOGIN PASSWORD '9389884141ecaf04';
CREATE USER finance_user WITH LOGIN PASSWORD 'a02308ce58c92131';
```

161

Across the business, we'll be making and taking orders for different things:

- **Retail** – Taking customer orders.

- **Roasting** – Making orders for raw materials and taking orders from the retail side of the business (e.g., a warehouse that fulfills online orders needs roasted coffee beans). We'll only create tables for making orders in this example for simplicity.

- **Finance** – Reconciling customer orders to online sales and roasting orders to company inventory. We'll ignore the need for the finance to make orders for anything they need for now.

Knowing that we'll need to conceptualize multiple order types, it's clear that creating schemas will simplify this. Let's create some schemas and database objects now. I won't create the roasting or finance schemas to keep things simple, as we can cover various types of testing by having just the retail schema.

Let's create the retail schema now. The retail schema will hold all of the database objects that are related to the retail operations of the business:

```
CREATE SCHEMA retail AUTHORIZATION retail_user;
```

Next, we'll create a table to hold our customer information:

```
CREATE TABLE retail.customer (
    id UUID PRIMARY KEY DEFAULT gen_random_uuid(),
    full_name STRING(255) NOT NULL,
    email STRING(320) NOT NULL,
    join_date TIMESTAMPTZ NOT NULL DEFAULT now()
);
```

Key design decisions:

- **Customer names** – Not everyone has a first and last name, so rather than asking for a separate first and last name, consider asking for a customer's full name instead.

- **join_date** – A question worth asking whenever you're dealing with time zones is whether you need to capture a timestamp as of a user's time, or the system's time. If it's the user's time, it makes sense to use the TIMESTAMPTZ data type, as this allows us to provide a user-specific time zone.

Next, we'll create a table to hold products:

```
CREATE TABLE retail.product (
     id UUID PRIMARY KEY DEFAULT gen_random_uuid(),
     name STRING(100) NOT NULL,
     sku STRING(16) NOT NULL
);
```

Key design decisions:

- **User Experience (UX)** – As with the order table, it's important to think of the experience of users *within* your company. If Stock-Keeping Units (SKUs) are used to identify products, make them easy to use and recall.

Rather than storing prices alongside products, we'll create a way of allowing product prices to change over time. For example, a customer might purchase a product while on sale. If they ask for a refund later, the business can't afford to lose money by refunding the product at a nonsale price.

The following table is a basic implementation of historical prices:

```
CREATE TABLE retail.product_price (
     id UUID PRIMARY KEY DEFAULT gen_random_uuid(),
     product_id UUID NOT NULL REFERENCES retail.product(id),
     amount DECIMAL NOT NULL,
     start_date TIMESTAMPTZ NOT NULL,
     end_date TIMESTAMPTZ
);
```

Key design decisions:

- **Simplicity** – To keep things straightforward, the business has decided to deal exclusively in one currency. As a result, I won't explicitly store currencies for now.

- **Correctness** – There are opposing schools of thought about whether decimals or integers should be used to store monetary values. Rounding errors may surface if calculations use floating-point numbers, so some prefer to use integers and only convert them to decimals for calculations temporarily in their code. This way, they can control how decimal values get rounded. As I won't perform any calculations, I've decided to keep things simple and use decimal.

- **Flexibility** – By storing product prices outside of the products table, we have flexibility with pricing. By including a start_date and end_date for a price, we can schedule price changes without updating them manually.

Next, we'll create a table to hold customer order information:

```
CREATE TABLE retail.order (
    id UUID PRIMARY KEY DEFAULT gen_random_uuid(),
    reference STRING(16) NOT NULL,
    customer_id UUID NOT NULL REFERENCES retail.customer(id),
    delivery_instructions STRING(255),
    order_date TIMESTAMPTZ NOT NULL DEFAULT now()
);
```

Key design decisions:

- **User Experience (UX)** – Consider your user's experience if presented with a UUID order number. If they're required to type or speak in a UUID when going through customer support, this could sour their experience. Instead, create short, easy-to-read identifiers for them.

Each order can contain multiple products, and each can appear in multiple orders. We'll resolve this many-to-many relationship with a third table:

```
CREATE TABLE retail.product_order (
    order_id UUID NOT NULL REFERENCES retail.order(id),
    product_id UUID NOT NULL REFERENCES retail.product(id),
    product_price_id UUID NOT NULL REFERENCES retail.product_price(id)
);
```

Following a conversation with the finance department, we've learned that members of their team will need to have access to objects in the retail schema for generating end-of-day reports, etc. Currently, if they try to access the objects of the retail schema, they won't see anything:

```
$ cockroach sql \
    --certs-dir=certs \
    --url "postgres://finance_user:a02308ce58c92131@localhost:26257/bean_
        about_town" \
    --execute "SELECT COUNT(*) FROM retail.order"
ERROR: user finance_user does not have SELECT privilege on relation order
```

Granting them USAGE and SELECT permissions on the retail schema objects will rectify this:

```
GRANT SELECT, INSERT, UPDATE, DELETE ON retail.* TO retail_user;
GRANT SELECT ON retail.* TO retail_user;

GRANT USAGE ON SCHEMA retail TO finance_user;
GRANT SELECT ON retail.* TO finance_user;
```

Functional Testing

Functional testing asserts that the database satisfies business requirements and use cases. We can run functional tests from either a user perspective (Black Box) or with a deeper understanding and direct access to the database (White Box). We'll go through each type of testing now.

To keep complexity from spiralling, I'll limit the tests to cover the retail schema.

Black Box Testing

Black Box testing tests the database from a user's perspective. No assumptions are made as to the database's internal structure, so tests can either happen via a UI or an API. I'll provide a simple API to abstract us from the database, as we don't have either. I'll use the Crystal driver from Chapter 5 to keep things succinct.

Before we begin, let's take a look at the use cases we'll need to implement for this test:

- **Create customer** – Insert a new customer into the database and return their ID.

- **Get customer** – Select a customer from the database by their ID.

- **Create Product with prices** – Insert a product and a collection of prices for it.

- **Get products** – Select a list of every product in the database.

- **Place order** – Insert a customer order for a list of products.

Create a Simple Application

First, create the scaffolding for the application with the following commands:

```
$ crystal init app api
$ cd api
```

Next, bring in the dependencies we'll need for this application by adding them to the shard.yml file and installing them:

```
dependencies:
  kemal:
    github: kemalcr/kemal
  pg:
    github: will/crystal-pg
$ shards install
```

With the dependencies installed, we're ready to write our API. As with the example code from Chapter 5, this code is nowhere near production quality and is provided to act as a mechanism for Black Box testing.

Let's start by importing some modules:

```
require "kemal"
require "db"
require "pg"
require "json"
require "uuid"
require "uuid/json"
```

Next, we'll create a connection to the database. Note that this connection will be in cleartext, which is not what you'd want for production use cases:

```
db = PG.connect "postgres://retail_user:7efd7222dfdfb107@localhost:26257/
bean_about_town?auth_methods=cleartext"
```

Now we're ready to wire up our API handlers. Let's start with a filter middleware handler that will attach a JSON Content-Type header to all responses. This will run before all of our handers execute and will add the correct Content-Type header to all responses:

```
before_all do |env|
  env.response.content_type = "application/json"
end
```

Next, we'll add a POST request handler to insert customers. This handler will

- Read full_name and email string values from a JSON request body

- Insert them into the retail.customer table

- Return the customer's ID and join_date

```
post "/customers" do |env|
  full_name = env.params.json["full_name"].as(String)
  email = env.params.json["email"].as(String)

  id, join_date =
    db.query_one "INSERT INTO retail.customer (full_name, email)
                  VALUES ($1, $2)
                  RETURNING id, join_date", full_name, email, as: {
                  UUID, Time }

  { "id": id, "join_date": join_date }.to_json
end
```

Next, we'll add a GET request handler to select customers by their IDs. This handler will

- Read an ID from the request URL path

- Select a customer out of the database with a matching ID

- Return a JSON object that represents the user

```
get "/customers/:id" do |env|
  id = env.params.url["id"]
  full_name, email, join_date =
```

```
    db.query_one "SELECT full_name, email, join_date FROM retail.customer
                WHERE id = $1
                LIMIT 1", id, as: { String, String, Time }
  { "id": id, "full_name": full_name, "email": email, "join_date": join_
  date }.to_json
end
```

Now we'll move onto products. Let's add a POST request endpoint to insert a product and its prices. This handler will

- Parse a product object from the request body

- Begin a transaction that will

  - Insert a product into the product table

  - Insert the prices for that product into the produce_price table

- Commit the transaction

- Return the product's ID

As we're reading an object from the request, I've created two classes: a Product class that will hold the top-level information of the product and a ProductPrice class that will contain a single, optionally expirable price for that product.

```
class Product
  include JSON::Serializable

  def initialize(@name : String, @sku : String)
    @prices = Array(ProductPrice).new
  end

  property id : UUID?
  property name : String
  property sku : String
  property prices : Array(ProductPrice)
end

class ProductPrice
  include JSON::Serializable
```

```
  def initialize(@id : UUID, @amount : Float64)
  end

  property id : UUID?
  property amount : Float64
  property start_date : Time?
  property end_date : Time?
end

post "/products" do |env|
  request = Product.from_json env.request.body.not_nil!

  id = UUID.empty
  db.transaction do |tx|
    id = tx.connection.query_one "INSERT INTO retail.product (name, sku)
                                  VALUES ($1, $2)
                                  RETURNING id", request.name, request.sku,
                                  as: { UUID }

    request.prices.each do |price|
      tx.connection.exec "INSERT INTO retail.product_price (product_id,
      amount, start_date, end_date)
                          VALUES ($1, $2, $3, $4)", id, price.amount,
                          price.start_date, price.end_date
    end
  end

  { "id": id }.to_json
end
```

As with the customer handler, we'll add a GET request handler for products too. This handler will

- Select the lowest active price for each product. This is defined as the lowest price for a product that has a start_date that's not in the future and either an end_date in the future or no end_date.

- Build up a collection of products found.

- Return the products as a JSON array.

```
get "/products" do |env|
  products = Array(Product).new
  db.query "WITH min_product_price AS (
             SELECT DISTINCT ON(product_id) product_id, id, min(amount)
             AS amount
             FROM retail.product_price
             WHERE start_date <= now()
             AND (end_date >= now() OR end_date IS NULL)
             GROUP BY id
             ORDER BY product_id, amount
           )
           SELECT p.id, p.name, p.sku, pp.id, pp.amount FROM min_product_
           price pp
           JOIN retail.product p ON pp.product_id = p.id" do |rs|
    rs.each do
      product_id, name, sku, price_id, amount = rs.read(UUID, String,
      String, UUID, PG::Numeric)
      product = Product.new(name, sku)
      product.id = product_id
      product.prices << ProductPrice.new(price_id, amount.to_f)
      products << product
    end
  end

  products.to_json
end
```

The next handler we'll create is a POST request handler to insert orders. As with the product POST handler, we'll capture a JSON request from the caller, so we will introduce a new class to handle the serialization. This handler will

- Parse an order object from the request body

- Generate a short customer reference number

- Begin a transaction that will

  - Insert an order into the order table

  - Insert the products and paid price into the product_order table

- Close the transaction

- Return the order ID and customer reference number

```
class Order
  include JSON::Serializable

  property id : UUID?
  property customer_id : UUID
  property delivery_instructions : String?
  property products : Hash(UUID, UUID)
end

post "/orders" do |env|
  request = Order.from_json env.request.body.not_nil!

  id = UUID.empty
  ref = ('A'..'Z').to_a.shuffle(Random::Secure)[0, 8].join

  db.transaction do |tx|
    id = tx.connection.query_one "INSERT INTO retail.order (reference,
    customer_id, delivery_instructions)
                               VALUES ($1, $2, $3)
                               RETURNING id", ref, request.customer_
                               id, request.delivery_instructions, as:
                               { UUID }

    request.products.each do |product_id, price_id|
      tx.connection.exec "INSERT INTO retail.product_order (order_id,
      product_id, product_price_id)
                               VALUES ($1, $2, $3)", id, product_id, price_id
    end
  end

  { "id": id }.to_json
end
```

The last handler we'll create is a GET request handler to select orders for a given customer ID. This handler will

- Read a customer ID from the request URL path

- Use the customer ID to select all of their orders

- Iterate through the results, building up a collection of orders with products

- Return an array of orders

```
class Order
  include JSON::Serializable

  def initialize(@id, @reference, @customer_id, @date, @delivery_
  instructions)
    @products = Hash(String, Float64).new
  end

  property id : UUID
  property reference : String
  property customer_id : UUID
  property date : Time
  property delivery_instructions : String
  property products : Hash(String, Float64)
end

get "/customers/:id/orders" do |env|
  customer_id = UUID.new(env.params.url["id"])

  orders = Hash(UUID, Order).new
  db.query "SELECT o.id, o.reference, o.delivery_instructions, order_date,
  p.name, pp.amount
          FROM retail.order o
          JOIN retail.product_order po ON o.id = po.order_id
          JOIN retail.product_price pp on po.product_price_id = pp.id
          JOIN retail.product p ON po.product_id = p.id
          WHERE o.customer_id = $1", customer_id do |rs|
      rs.each do
```

```
    id, ref, instructions, date, product, amount =
      rs.read(UUID, String, String, Time, String, PG::Numeric)

    unless orders.has_key? id
      orders[id] = Order.new(id, ref, customer_id, date, instructions)
    end

    orders[id].products[product] = amount.to_f
  end
end

orders.values.to_json
end
```

All that's left to do now is to start the API server listening. This code will

- Start the Kemal web server on port 3000

```
  Kemal.run
```

With the code in place, we can start the server with the following command:

```
$ crystal run src/api.cr
[development] Kemal is ready to lead at http://0.0.0.0:3000
```

Test the Application

Let's write some cURL commands to test the API (and, in doing so, the database). During this phase of testing, we'll need to assert not only that the database behaves as expected when given expected data but also that it behaves as expected when given *unexpected* data. These are commonly referred to as Boundary Tests.

In this section, we'll go through each of our use cases to assert the database can support them. Let's start by creating a customer:

```
$ curl -X POST 'localhost:3000/customers' \
    -H 'Content-Type: application/json' \
    -d '{
        "full_name": "Malala Yousafzai",
        "email": "malala.yousafzai@example.com"
    }'
{"id":"7d640140-5581-41cf-a9db-0bccaf90f2de","join_date":"2022-01-20T18:26:18Z"}
```

This covers the happy path: a sensibly sized name and email address. Does our database support unicode characters? Let's find out:

```
$ curl -X POST 'localhost:3000/customers' \
    -H 'Content-Type: application/json' \
    -d '{
        "full_name": "Надéжда Андрéевна Толокóнникова",
        "email": "nadya.tolokno@example.com"
    }'
{"id":"85f05ac3-931f-4417-a6ae-1403468a2c10","join_date":"2022-01-20T18:26:34Z"}
```

Seems to! How about long names? Does the database reject full names that are greater than the maximum 255 length we defined?

```
$ curl -X POST 'localhost:3000/customers' \
    -H 'Content-Type: application/json' \
    -d '{
        "full_name": "aaaaaaaaaabbbbbbbbbbcccccccccccddddddddddeeeeeeeeeeaaaa
        aaaaaabbbbbbbbbbcccccccccccddddddddddeeeeeeeeeeaaaaaaaaaabbbbbbbbbbcc
        cccccccddddddddddeeeeeeeeeeaaaaaaaaaabbbbbbbbbbcccccccccccdddddddddd
        eeeeeeeeeeaaaaaaaaaabbbbbbbbbbcccccccccccddddddddddeeeeeeeeeefffffg",
        "email": "full_name@example.com"
    }'
...ERROR OMITTED
```

The server is absent of any error handling, but the logs confirm that our attempt to store a customer with a 256-character-long full_name failed:

```
Exception: value too long for type STRING(255) (PQ::PQError)
```

What about the boundary case of a 255-character-long full_name?

```
$ curl -X POST 'localhost:3000/customers' \
    -H 'Content-Type: application/json' \
    -d '{
        "full_name": "aaaaaaaaaabbbbbbbbbbcccccccccccddddddddddeeeeeeeeeeaaaa
        aaaaaabbbbbbbbbbcccccccccccddddddddddeeeeeeeeeeaaaaaaaaaabbbbbbbbbbcc
        cccccccddddddddddeeeeeeeeeeaaaaaaaaaabbbbbbbbbbcccccccccccdddddddddd
        eeeeeeeeeeaaaaaaaaaabbbbbbbbbbcccccccccccddddddddddeeeeeeeeeefffff",
```

```
        "email": "full_name@example.com"
    }'
{"id":"d93bedb4-3e59-4bd5-b018-b6d89d688904","join_
date":"2022-01-20T18:26:53Z"}
```

Ignoring email addresses for now, our create customer use case is looking good, and it seems that our database is satisfying the basics of this use case. Let's move onto the get customer use case now.

First, we'll make a request to fetch an existing customer:

```
$ curl -X GET 'localhost:3000/customers/85f05ac3-931f-4417-
a6ae-1403468a2c10'
{"id":"85f05ac3-931f-4417-a6ae-1403468a2c10","full_name":"Надéжда
Андрéевна Толокóнникова","email":"nadya.tolokno@example.com","join_
date":"2022-01-20T18:26:34Z"}
```

This returns the data we originally inserted for this user. There are obviously no security checks around who are allowed to make requests for specific users, but from the perspective of the database, this is our happy path test satisfied. How about unhappy paths? Let's try omitting the customer ID in the URL path, searching for a customer by a nonexistent ID, and searching for a customer with a malformatted UUID. For these tests, I'll limit the response to just the headers, as without proper error handling, we'll receive an HTML page response.

```
curl -I -X GET localhost:3000/customers/
HTTP/1.1 404 Not Found
Connection: keep-alive
X-Powered-By: Kemal
Content-Type: text/html
Transfer-Encoding: chunked
```

In the response to a request without an ID in the path, we receive a 404 because the path is expecting /customers/{CUSTOMER_ID}. This test has not reached the database, which is expected.

```
curl -I -X GET localhost:3000/customers/df24592d-62dd-4876-
b54a-405be8614aaf
HTTP/1.1 500 Internal Server Error
```

```
Connection: keep-alive
X-Powered-By: Kemal
Content-Type: text/html
Transfer-Encoding: chunked
```

In the response to a request for a nonexistent ID, we receive a 500 because of insufficient exception handling around the database call. Inspecting the server logs, we can see that the request yielded no results. Again, an expected result:

```
Exception: no results (DB::NoResultsError)
```

```
curl -I -X GET localhost:3000/customers/a
HTTP/1.1 500 Internal Server Error
Connection: keep-alive
X-Powered-By: Kemal
Content-Type: text/html
Transfer-Encoding: chunked
```

In the response to a request with a malformatted customer ID, we receive a 500. Again, this is due to insufficient error handling around the database call. Inspecting the server logs again reveals the underlying cause of the response we received. This request also made it to the database but returned an error during query preparation. An expected result once more:

```
Exception: error in argument for $1: could not parse string "a" as uuid
(PQ::PQError)
```

Onto the creation of products. This scenario provides our first test of a multistatement transaction. In this transaction, we insert a product and then insert some prices using the previously inserted product ID. Let's make a request:

```
$ curl -X POST 'localhost:3000/products' \
-d '{
    "name": "Where Have You Bean All My Life?",
    "sku": "L2JM9XAO",
    "prices": [
        { "amount": 6.00, "start_date": "2022-01-01T09:00:00Z", "end_date":
        "2022-01-01T10:00:00Z" },
```

```
        { "amount": 12.00, "start_date": "2022-01-01T09:00:00Z" }
    ]
}'
{"id":"d77bfea2-f0df-4da9-aeef-7c8d9c362e38"}
```

We've given two prices to the product we've just inserted: a full price of 12.00 and a half price of 6.00. The half price offer is set to expire one hour after it becomes available, so at the time of testing, I would expect the price for this product to be 12.00 for every request.

We also want to assert that if there are multiple active prices, we always returned the cheapest:

```
$ curl -X POST 'localhost:3000/products' \
-d '{
    "name": "Has Bean",
    "sku": "10LEMX05",
    "prices": [
        { "amount": 6.00, "start_date": "2022-01-02T09:00:00Z", "end_date":
        "2022-01-02T10:00:00Z" },
        { "amount": 10.00, "start_date": "2022-01-01T09:00:00Z" },
        { "amount": 12.00, "start_date": "2022-01-01T09:00:00Z" }
    ]
}'
{"id":"386e841e-4da8-4688-82a4-71d6fbb369fa"}
```

Rather than run a suite of explorative tests against this endpoint, let's skip ahead to fetching the product and its prices:

```
$ curl -X GET 'localhost:3000/products'
[
{"id":"386e841e-4da8-4688-82a4-71d6fbb369fa","name":"Has Bean","sku":
"10LEMX05","prices":[{"id":"cc71e211-abc6-42d5-8f59-d357042334b0",
"amount":10.0}]},
{"id":"d77bfea2-f0df-4da9-aeef-7c8d9c362e38","name":"Where Have You Bean
All My Life?","sku":"L2JM9XAO","prices":[{"id":"cbdc9d9c-a987-4655-b3f8-6b9
b2ec9c50e","amount":12.0}]}
]
```

In the response body (which I've formatted slightly for readability), we can see that our two products have been returned and that neither the expired sale price nor the more expensive active price appears.

Next, let's place an order and check the database behavior with our next multistatement transaction call. In this scenario, we'll create an order and then use its ID to insert rows into the product_order table:

```
$ curl -X POST 'localhost:3000/orders' \
-d '{
  "customer_id": "85f05ac3-931f-4417-a6ae-1403468a2c10",
  "delivery_instructions": "Please leave package behind the green bin.",
  "products": {
    "386e841e-4da8-4688-82a4-71d6fbb369fa": "cc71e211-abc6-42d5-8f59-
    d357042334b0",
    "d77bfea2-f0df-4da9-aeef-7c8d9c362e38": "cbdc9d9c-a987-4655-
    b3f8-6b9b2ec9c50e"
  }
}'
{"id":"3ad9469a-50ec-4773-bc50-1c92209078de","reference":"NIAXGBQP"}
```

Let's check that the order was inserted successfully by making a request the endpoint that returns a customer's orders:

```
$ curl -X GET localhost:3000/customers/85f05ac3-931f-4417-
a6ae-1403468a2c10/orders
[{"id":"93bff9af-5794-47a5-94e5-18e8a9832c41","reference":"GDCQONIR","
customer_id":"85f05ac3-931f-4417-a6ae-1403468a2c10","date":"2022-01-20
T18:32:45Z","delivery_instructions":"Please leave package behind the
green bin.","products":{"Has Bean":10.0,"Where Have You Bean All My
Life?":12.0}}]
```

In the response body, we can see that all of the order fields are included, along with the correct products and prices.

Testing with Application Code

Up to now, we've tested our API as a black box itself. What if we want to test just the database as the black box from within our application's own test suite? Let's see how CockroachDB can be included in your local test environment with Docker Compose.

For this example, we're going to need a few files:

- **docker-compose.yml** – Holds the Docker services that will run as part of our combined application and database test suite. Namely, a service for our application code and a service for CockroachDB.

- **Dockerfile** – A file that will package our application test binary into a Docker image.

- **main_test.go** – Our application test code. For this example, I'm using Go.

Let's begin! We'll start by preparing a directory to house our tests with a few commands:

```
$ mkdir db_tests
$ cd db_tests
$ go mod init dbtests
```

Next, we'll pull in the database dependency that will enable database interaction:

```
$ go get -u github.com/jackc/pgx
```

Next, we'll create the Go code that will connect to the database and run some unit tests. As this file lives in isolation of any other Go code, there are no dependencies to other self-managed Go modules. In this code, we will

- Read a flag from the command line, indicating whether database tests should be included or not (defaults to `false`)

- If database tests are flagged to run:

  - Read a connection string from the environment.

  - Attempt to connect to the database in a simple back-off loop while the database is launching.

  - Close the database connection once all tests have completed.

179

- Run unit tests and capture a status code indicating whether the tests passed or failed.

- Exit the application with the status code received from the test run.

- Note that the TestADatabaseInteraction function will only execute if the database flag has been provided.

```go
package main

import (
        "context"
        "flag"
        "log"
        "os"
        "testing"
        "time"

        "github.com/jackc/pgx/v4/pgxpool"
)

var (
        dbTests *bool
        db      *pgxpool.Pool
)

func TestMain(m *testing.M) {
        dbTests = flag.Bool("db", false, "run database tests")
        flag.Parse()

        if *dbTests {
                connStr, ok := os.LookupEnv("CONN_STR")
                if !ok {
                        log.Fatal("connection string env var not found")
                }

                if err := waitForDB(connStr); err != nil {
                        log.Fatalf("error waiting for database: %v", err)
                }
        }
```

```go
        code := m.Run()

        if *dbTests {
                db.Close()
        }

        os.Exit(code)
}

func waitForDB(connStr string) error {
        var err error
        for i := 1; i <= 10; i++ {
                db, err = pgxpool.Connect(context.Background(), connStr)
                if err != nil {
                        log.Printf("error connecting to database: %v", err)
                        time.Sleep(time.Second * time.Duration(i))
                }
        }

        return err
}

func TestADatabaseInteraction(t *testing.T) {
        if !*dbTests {
                t.SkipNow()
        }

        t.Log("running database test")
}

func TestANonDatabaseInteraction(t *testing.T) {
        t.Log("running non-database test")
}
```

Note that at this point, we'll be able to run all tests that don't require a database connection with the following command:

```
$ go test ./... -v
=== RUN   TestADatabaseInteraction
--- SKIP: TestADatabaseInteraction (0.00s)
```

181

```
=== RUN    TestANonDatabaseInteraction
    main_test.go:65: running non-database test
--- PASS: TestANonDatabaseInteraction (0.00s)
PASS
ok
```

Next, we'll package up the application into a Docker image, so it can be executed alongside CockroachDB in a Docker Compose environment. This can be very simple because we'll be executing a Linux-compatible executable that will exist in the /app directory.

```
FROM alpine:latest
COPY . /app
WORKDIR /app
```

With our code (and this Dockerfile) in place, we can build a Docker image ready to use in Docker Compose. The first command will build a test executable for a Linux machine called "crdb-test". The second command will bundle our current working directory (including the test executable) into the /app directory:

```
$ GOOS=linux go test ./... -c -o crdb-test
$ docker build -t crdb-test .
```

The last file we'll create will be for Docker Compose. This file will create two services: one for CockroachDB and one for our test suite. In this file, we

- Create a cockroach_test service using the v21.2.4 version of the CockroachDB Docker image that will

  - Customize its startup command to run just a single node, so it doesn't wait for an initialization command

  - Not expose CockroachDB's default port of 26257, as there's no need to access CockroachDB from the host machine

  - Suppress logs, meaning our test suite logs are the only output we see

- Create an app_test service using the Docker image we built in the previous step:

  - Pass an environment variable called CONN_STR to the container, containing the information required to connect to the database. Note that we use the name of the cockroach_test service instead of "localhost" because of the way Docker networking works.

  - Pass the -db command-line argument to ensure that database tests run.

  - Pass the -test.v command-line argument to ensure that we receive verbose logging. With this set, we'll see each function that runs.

  - Set the working directory for the container to the directory where the test executable resides.

  - Mark the container as being dependent on the cockroach_ test service

We'll run both of the containers in a Docker bridge network called app-network so that they can talk to each other.

```yaml
version: '3'

services:
  cockroach_test:
    image: cockroachdb/cockroach:v21.2.4
    command: start-single-node --insecure
    logging:
      driver: none
    networks:
    - app-network

  app_test:
    image: crdb-test:latest
    environment:
      CONN_STR: postgres://root@cockroach_test:26257/
      defaultdb?sslmode=disable
    command: ./crdb-test -db -test.v
```

```
    working_dir: /app
    depends_on:
    - cockroach_test
    networks:
    - app-network

networks:
  app-network:
    driver: bridge
```

With everything in place, we can kick off the full database test with the following command:

```
$ docker-compose up --abort-on-container-exit --force-recreate
Recreating app_cockroach_test_1 ... done
Recreating app_app_test_1        ... done
Attaching to app_app_test_1
app_test_1        | === RUN    TestADatabaseInteraction
app_test_1        |     main_test.go:61: running database test
app_test_1        | --- PASS: TestADatabaseInteraction (0.00s)
app_test_1        | === RUN    TestANonDatabaseInteraction
app_test_1        |     main_test.go:65: running non-database test
app_test_1        | --- PASS: TestANonDatabaseInteraction (0.00s)
app_test_1        | PASS
app_app_test_1 exited with code 0
Aborting on container exit...
Stopping app_cockroach_test_1   ... done
```

As we can see, both the database and the nondatabase test ran as expected. After the app_test service container finishes, both the app_test and the cockroach_test containers exit.

White Box Testing

White Box testing involves testing everything a user wouldn't normally see and includes things like referential integrity checks, index query plan analysis, and default value assignment checks. Let's go through some of these now.

Referential Integrity Checks

Referential integrity checks ensure that intertable dependencies prevent unexpected destructive operations. Let's perform a few destructive operations to ensure the referential integrity of our database.

First, we'll try to delete everything from the retail.order, retail.product, and retail.product_price tables. Something that – without due care – could result in a bad day in the office:

```
DELETE FROM retail.order WHERE true;
ERROR: delete on table "order" violates foreign key constraint "fk_order_
id_ref_order" on table "product_order"
SQLSTATE: 23503
DETAIL: Key (id)=('93bff9af-5794-47a5-94e5-18e8a9832c41') is still
referenced from table "product_order".
CONSTRAINT: fk_order_id_ref_order

DELETE FROM retail.product_price WHERE true;
ERROR: delete on table "product_price" violates foreign key constraint "fk_
product_price_id_ref_product_price" on table "product_order"
SQLSTATE: 23503
DETAIL: Key (id)=('cbdc9d9c-a987-4655-b3f8-6b9b2ec9c50e') is still
referenced from table "product_order".
CONSTRAINT: fk_product_price_id_ref_product_price

DELETE FROM retail.product WHERE true;
ERROR: delete on table "product" violates foreign key constraint "fk_
product_id_ref_product" on table "product_price"
SQLSTATE: 23503
DETAIL: Key (id)=('386e841e-4da8-4688-82a4-71d6fbb369fa') is still
referenced from table "product_price".
CONSTRAINT: fk_product_id_ref_product
```

Without these reference checks, we would have created orphaned data in the referencing tables. It's important to note that without proper permissions, we could still inadvertently delete data from the retail.customer and retail.product_order tables. Still, we can rest assured that checks are in place for the remaining tables.

Indexes and Query Plans

Onto indexes. Let's check that the indexes in the tables we're querying are sufficient to query data without requiring full table scans. We'll go through each of the SELECT queries in the API code to see how optimized they are and determine what we can do to improve their performance.

The first query we'll look at fetches a customer by their ID:

```
EXPLAIN SELECT full_name, email, join_date FROM retail.customer
WHERE id = '85f05ac3-931f-4417-a6ae-1403468a2c10'
LIMIT 1;
                                    info
---------------------------------------------------------------------------
  distribution: local
  vectorized: true

  • scan
    estimated row count: 1 (33% of the table; stats collected 28
    minutes ago)
    table: customer@primary
    spans: [/'85f05ac3-931f-4417-a6ae-1403468a2c10' - /'85f05ac3-931f-4417-
    a6ae-1403468a2c10']
```

Of the three items in the table, we've scanned just the one with the ID we're interested in (or 33% of the table). The ID is the table's primary key, so it's already indexed and nice and efficient. Note that while I don't need to include the LIMIT 1 expression (as there'll only be one instance of this ID in the table), I think it's a safe and sensible habit if you further restrict your queries to the number of expected rows you'd like returned.

```
EXPLAIN WITH min_product_price AS (
  SELECT DISTINCT ON(product_id) product_id, id, min(amount) AS amount
  FROM retail.product_price
  WHERE start_date <= now()
  AND (end_date >= now() OR end_date IS NULL)
  GROUP BY id
  ORDER BY product_id, amount
)
```

```
SELECT p.id, p.name, p.sku, pp.id price_id, pp.amount FROM min_product_
price pp
JOIN retail.product p ON pp.product_id = p.id
                                info
-------------------------------------------------------------------------------
  distribution: full
  vectorized: true

  • lookup join
  | estimated row count: 2
  | table: product@primary
  | equality: (product_id) = (id)
  | equality cols are key
  |
  └─── • render
       | estimated row count: 3
       |
       └─── • distinct
            | estimated row count: 3
            | distinct on: any_not_null
            |
            └─── • sort
                 | estimated row count: 3
                 | order: +min
                 |
                 └─── • group
                      | estimated row count: 3
                      | group by: id
                      | ordered: +id
                      |
                      └─── • filter
                           | estimated row count: 3
                           | filter: (start_date <= '2022-01-24
                             19:14:54.499657+00:00') AND ((end_date >=
                             '2022-01-24 19:14:54.499657+00:00') OR (end_date
                             IS NULL))
```

```
        |
        └──── • scan
                estimated row count: 5 (100% of the table;
                stats collected 33 minutes ago)
                table: product_price@primary
                spans: FULL SCAN
```

Oh dear! From the FULL SCAN, it's clear we're missing some indexes. CockroachDB has highlighted the start_date <= filter, the end_date >= filter, and the end_date IS NULL filter as candidates for this issue. Unless fixed, the performance of this query will continue to degrade as the table grows.

Let's add some indexes to these columns to make our query more efficient.

```
CREATE INDEX start_date_asc_idx ON retail.product_price(start_date ASC);
CREATE INDEX end_date_desc_idx ON retail.product_price(end_date DESC);
```

As the start_date filter checks that start_date column values are less than or equal to a given value, I've provided the default ASC sort order (this could be omitted but I've kept it in to make it obvious). As the end_date filter checks that end_date column values are greater than or equal to a given value, I've provided the DESC sort order.

Let's try the query again with these indexes in place:

```
EXPLAIN WITH min_product_price AS (
  SELECT DISTINCT ON(product_id) product_id, id, min(amount) AS amount
  FROM retail.product_price
  WHERE start_date <= now()
  AND (end_date >= now() OR end_date IS NULL)
  GROUP BY id
  ORDER BY product_id, amount
)
SELECT p.id, p.name, p.sku, pp.id price_id, pp.amount FROM min_product_
price pp
JOIN retail.product p ON pp.product_id = p.id
                                        info
-----------------------------------------------------------------------
  distribution: full
  vectorized: true
```

```
• lookup join
│ estimated row count: 2
│ table: product@primary
│ equality: (product_id) = (id)
│ equality cols are key
│
└── • render
    │ estimated row count: 3
    │
    └── • distinct
        │ estimated row count: 3
        │ distinct on: any_not_null
        │
        └── • sort
            │ estimated row count: 3
            │ order: +min
            │
            └── • group
                │ estimated row count: 3
                │ group by: id
                │ ordered: +id
                │
                └── • filter
                    │ estimated row count: 3
                    │ filter: start_date <= '2022-01-24
                    │   19:47:57.059747+00:00'
                    │
                    └── • index join
                        │ estimated row count: 0
                        │ table: product_price@primary
                        │
                        └── • sort
                            │ estimated row count: 0
                            │ order: +id
                            │
                            └── • scan
```

```
                              estimated row count: 0 (<0.01% of the
                              table; stats collected 16 minutes ago)
                              table: product_price@end_date_desc_idx
                              spans: [ - /'2022-01-24
                              19:47:57.059747+00:00'] [/NULL - /NULL]
```

Much better! Let's move on.

```
EXPLAIN SELECT o.id, o.reference, o.delivery_instructions, order_date,
p.name, pp.amount
FROM retail.order o
JOIN retail.product_order po ON o.id = po.order_id
JOIN retail.product_price pp on po.product_price_id = pp.id
JOIN retail.product p ON po.product_id = p.id
WHERE o.customer_id = '85f05ac3-931f-4417-a6ae-1403468a2c10';
                                        info
-------------------------------------------------------------------------------
  distribution: full
  vectorized: true

  • lookup join
  | estimated row count: 2
  | table: product@primary
  | equality: (product_id) = (id)
  | equality cols are key
  |
  └── • lookup join
      | estimated row count: 2
      | table: product_price@primary
      | equality: (product_price_id) = (id)
      | equality cols are key
      |
      └── • lookup join
          | estimated row count: 2
          | table: order@primary
          | equality: (order_id) = (id)
```

```
| equality cols are key
| pred: customer_id = '85f05ac3-931f-4417-a6ae-1403468a2c10'
|
└── • scan
        estimated row count: 2 (100% of the table; stats collected
        1 hour ago)
        table: product_order@primary
        spans: FULL SCAN
```

Another full table scan! The reason for this full table scan, however, is the multiple table joins with missing indexes, rather than a single table with a missing index. Let's add indexes to the columns that are participating in the join and rerun the explain:

```
CREATE INDEX order_customer_id_idx ON retail.order(customer_id);
CREATE INDEX product_order_order_id_idx ON retail.product_order(order_id);
CREATE INDEX product_price_product_id_idx ON retail.product_
price(product_id);

EXPLAIN SELECT o.id, o.reference, o.delivery_instructions, order_date,
p.name, pp.amount
FROM retail.order o
JOIN retail.product_order po ON o.id = po.order_id
JOIN retail.product_price pp on po.product_price_id = pp.id
JOIN retail.product p ON po.product_id = p.id
WHERE o.customer_id = '85f05ac3-931f-4417-a6ae-1403468a2c10';
                                      info
--------------------------------------------------------------------------------
  distribution: local
  vectorized: true

  • lookup join
  | estimated row count: 1
  | table: product_price@primary
  | equality: (product_price_id) = (id)
  | equality cols are key
  |
  └── • lookup join
```

```
| estimated row count: 0
| table: product@primary
| equality: (product_id) = (id)
| equality cols are key
|
└── • lookup join
    | table: product_order@primary
    | equality: (rowid) = (rowid)
    | equality cols are key
    |
    └── • lookup join
        | estimated row count: 0
        | table: product_order@product_order_order_id_idx
        | equality: (id) = (order_id)
        |
        └── • index join
            | estimated row count: 0
            | table: order@primary
            |
            └── • scan
                estimated row count: 0 (<0.01% of the table; stats
                collected 4 minutes ago)
                table: order@order_customer_id_idx
                spans: [/'00088f1e-4f35-4629-a07c-5b9fc0c2bac7' -
                /'00088f1e-4f35-4629-a07c-5b9fc0c2bac7']
```

Much better. It's important to note that when writes occur against a table, locking occurs, leading to contention. To view where your database contention occurs, you can visit the /sql-activity?tab=Statements page of the Admin Console or run the following commands in the SQL shell. The first highlights contented for *tables* and the second highlights contended for *indexes*:

```
SELECT schema_name, table_name, num_contention_events FROM crdb_internal.
cluster_contended_tables;
```

schema_name	table_name	num_contention_events
retail	order	22
public	jobs	7
retail	product_order	6

```
SELECT schema_name, table_name, index_name, num_contention_events FROM
crdb_internal.cluster_contended_indexes;
```

schema_name	table_name	index_name	num_contention_events
retail	order	order_customer_id_idx	15
retail	product_order	primary	6

From this information, we can determine the contention hotspots in our database and deal with them. One way to reduce contention is to split operations into separate statements. Our API runs every statement to create products and orders in the same transaction, creating contention, especially if many statements execute. I prefer multirow DML[1] (Data Manipulation Language) over executing multiple statements in a more production-friendly environment. Consider the following INSERT statements. The first uses single-row DML to insert three records, while the second harnesses multirow DML. The outcome of using DML is fewer network round trips, less parsing of SQL statements, and less time for a locked row to increase contention on a table or index.

Single-row DML:

```
INSERT INTO a_table (a_column) VALUES ('1');
INSERT INTO a_table (a_column) VALUES ('2');
INSERT INTO a_table (a_column) VALUES ('3');
```

Multirow DML:

```
INSERT INTO a_table (a_column) VALUES ('1'), ('2'), ('3');
```

Depending on the language and driver you're using, you may be able to take advantage of reWriteBatchedInserts,[2] which will automatically convert single-row DML queries to multirow DML statements.

---

[1] www.cockroachlabs.com/blog/multi-row-dml
[2] www.cockroachlabs.com/docs/stable/build-a-java-app-with-cockroachdb.html

In the real world, I would keep the transaction and harness multirow DML to ensure that changes resulting from the insertion of products and prices get committed together, and if any error occurred, they are rolled back together, with no side effects or orphaned rows.

The API we've created is tiny and contains just a handful of queries, making this kind of White Box testing quick and painless. What if you performed hundreds or thousands of queries and didn't have time to check them all individually?

CockroachDB's SHOW FULL TABLE SCANS statement returns every statement that resulted in a full table scan and is available to admin users. Run this tool after a suite of automated or Black Box tests (and in production), and you'll see which queries you need to tune.

Nonfunctional Testing

Nonfunctional testing asserts that the database satisfies the *'ilities*: reliability, scalability, etc. In this section, we'll cover some of the most common types of nonfunctional testing you might come across when integrating CockroachDB.

Performance Testing

To get value from a performance test, we must first understand how the application will use our database. Which tables will be the most frequently used? What is the impact of calling them? Are there any client-side interactions that result in many database calls?

Let's start this section by understanding the client-side interactions and how they result in database calls. We'll do this by listing the interactions in descending order of expected call frequency:

- **Fetch all products** – This will invoke a fairly simple SELECT statement once per call. This statement could potentially return a lot of data.

- **Fetch a customer** – This will invoke a simple SELECT statement once per call. This request uses a primary key index, so it's inherently optimized.

- **Fetch customer orders** – This will invoke a simple SELECT statement using three joins.

- **Create a customer** – This will invoke a simple INSERT statement once per new customer.

- **Create an order** – Like the request to create a product, this will invoke at least one INSERT statement and a subsequent INSERT statement of each product ordered. All within a simple transaction.

- **Create a product** – This will invoke at least one INSERT statement and a subsequent INSERT statement for each product price. All within a simple transaction.

I'll use k6,[3] an open source load testing tool written in Go, and JavaScript scriptable, to simulate these transactions.

To keep things light, I'll implement just two k6 scripts. For the sake of brevity, I won't spend time simulating accurate user behavior:

- **products.js** – A script to insert multiple random products into the database via the API

- **customers.js** – A script to simulate a user browsing for products, placing an order, then checking the status of their order

First, let's create the products.js script to simulate a user creating products. This script will

- Make a POST request to the /products endpoint with a JSON body representing a product with a random name, SKU, and an active, random price

- Fail if the response status is not 200 (success)

- Fail if after running all of the test iterations, the error rate was greater than 1% or the request duration for the 95% percentile was greater than 100ms

```
import http from 'k6/http';
import { check } from 'k6';
import { randomString, randomIntBetween } from 'https://jslib.k6.io/k6-
utils/1.1.0/index.js';
```

---

[3] https://k6.io

```
const BASE_URL = 'http://localhost:3000';

export const options = {
  thresholds: {
    http_req_failed: ['rate<0.01'],
    http_req_duration: ['p(95)<100'],
  }
};

export default() => {
  const createResponse = http.post(
    `${BASE_URL}/products`,
    JSON.stringify({
      name: 'Name ' + randomString(16),
      sku: 'SKU ' + randomString(10),
      prices: [
        {
          amount: randomIntBetween(1, 100),
          start_date: addDays(new Date(), -10),
          end_date: addDays(new Date(), 10),
        }
      ]
    }),
    { headers: {'Content-Type': 'application/json'} }
  );

  check(createResponse, { 'create product response': (r) => r.status
  === 200 });
};

function addDays(date, days) {
  date.setDate(date.getDate() + days);
  return date;
}
```

Now, let's create the customers.js script to simulate a customer using the database via the API. This script will

- Make a POST request to the /customers endpoint with a JSON body that represents a customer with a random full_name and email

- Fail if the response status from creating the customer is not 200 (success)

- Capture the customer's ID from the response body JSON and pass it into the iteration loop. Within the iteration loop, we

  - Make two GET requests to the /products endpoint to simulate a customer browsing for products

  - Make a third GET request to the /products endpoint but this time, capturing an array of products

  - Pick a random product from the array of products

  - Make a POST request to the /orders endpoint with a JSON body that represents the customer's order and product

  - Make two GET requests to the /customers/{id}/orders endpoint to simulate the customer checking the status of their order

- Fail if after running all of the test iterations, the error rate was greater than 1% or the request duration for the 95% percentile was greater than 200ms

```
import http from 'k6/http';
import { check, group } from 'k6';
import { randomString, randomItem } from 'https://jslib.k6.io/k6-
utils/1.1.0/index.js';

const BASE_URL = 'http://localhost:3000';

export const options = {
  thresholds: {
    http_req_failed: ['rate<0.01'],
```

```
    http_req_duration: ['p(95)<200'],
  }
};

export function setup() {
  const name = randomString(16);
  const createResponse = http.post(
    `${BASE_URL}/customers`,
    JSON.stringify({
      full_name: 'Full Name ' + name,
      email: name + `@acme.com`
    }),
    { headers: {'Content-Type': 'application/json'} }
  );

  check(createResponse, { 'create customer response': (r) => r.status
  === 200 });

  return createResponse.json('id');
}

export default (id) => {
  group('make order', () => {
    // Simulate a customer browsing before placing an order.
    http.batch([
      ['GET', `${BASE_URL}/products`, null],
      ['GET', `${BASE_URL}/products`, null],
    ]);

    // Make a request and capture the response to extract a random
    product to buy.
    const productsResponse = http.get(
      `${BASE_URL}/products`,
    );

    const product = randomItem(productsResponse.json());
    const productId = product.id;
    const priceId = product.prices[0].id;
```

```
    // Place order.
    http.post(
      `${BASE_URL}/orders`,
      JSON.stringify({
        customer_id: id,
        products: { [productId]: priceId },
      }),
      { headers: {'Content-Type': 'application/json'} }
      );
    });

    // Simulate a customer checking their order status.
    group('check orders', () => {
      http.batch([
        ['GET', `${BASE_URL}/customers/${id}/orders`, null],
        ['GET', `${BASE_URL}/customers/${id}/orders`, null],
      ]);
    });
};
```

Time to run our simulations. First, let's kick off the products.js script and ask it to run for ten seconds. As we won't have many people entering products, I'll simulate just one user entering products (at five products per second; I didn't say they were an ordinary person).

```
$ k6 -u 1 -d 10m --rps 5 run products.js
running (10.0s), 0/1 VUs, 51 complete and 0 interrupted iterations
default ✓ [======================================] 1 VUs   10s

    ✓ create product response

    checks.........................: 100.00% ✓ 51        ✗ 0
    data_received..................: 8.2 kB   818 B/s
    data_sent......................: 15 kB    1.5 kB/s
  ✓ http_req_duration..............: avg=41.36ms   min=24.43ms
  med=37.63ms   max=114.66ms p(90)=67.91ms   p(95)=77.02ms
      { expected_response:true }...: avg=41.36ms   min=24.43ms
      med=37.63ms   max=114.66ms p(90)=67.91ms   p(95)=77.02ms
```

```
✓ http_req_failed.................: 0.00%    ✓ 0           ✗ 51
  iterations.....................: 51       5.077393/s
  vus............................: 1        min=1      max=1
  vus_max........................: 1        min=1      max=1
```

With that running, we'll kick off the customers.js script and ask it to run for ten seconds. I'll simulate just two customers for now, and they'll complete the full scenario as quickly as possible:

```
$ k6 -u 2 -d 10s run customer.js
running (10.0s), 0/2 VUs, 55 complete and 0 interrupted iterations
default ✓ [======================================] 2 VUs   10s

    ▮ setup

        ✓ create customer response

    ▮ make order

    ▮ check orders

    checks.........................: 100.00% ✓ 1          ✗ 0
    data_received..................: 55 MB    5.4 MB/s
    data_sent......................: 45 kB    4.5 kB/s
  ✓ http_req_duration..............: avg=41.88ms  min=27.75ms
     med=44.86ms  max=55.69ms  p(90)=50.78ms  p(95)=52.32ms
      { expected_response:true }...: avg=41.88ms  min=27.75ms
     med=44.86ms  max=55.69ms  p(90)=50.78ms  p(95)=52.32ms
  ✓ http_req_failed................: 0.00%    ✓ 0          ✗ 37
    iterations.....................: 37       4.99938/s
    vus............................: 1        min=1      max=1
    vus_max........................: 1        min=1      max=1
```

Scaling Up Your Test Environment

If you ran into issues running the preceding tests, it could be because your three-node CockroachDB cluster is being accessed via a single, "hot," node. To ramp up your test environment and introduce load balancing, I'll now create a local Dockerized cluster that sits behind an HAProxy, a container courtesy of the brilliant Tim Veil of Cockroach Labs.

Create a Docker Compose configuration file called docker-compose.yml with the following content. This file will

- Create three CockroachDB nodes that, open starting, will attempt to form a cluster together

- Create an HAProxy load balancer that will forward requests from the host machine to each of the CockroachDB nodes

```
services:

  node1:
    image: cockroachdb/cockroach:v21.2.4
    hostname: node1
    container_name: node1
    command: start --insecure --join=node1,node2,node3
    networks:
    - app-network

  node2:
    image: cockroachdb/cockroach:v21.2.4
    hostname: node2
    container_name: node2
    command: start --insecure --join=node1,node2,node3
    networks:
    - app-network

  node3:
    image: cockroachdb/cockroach:v21.2.4
    hostname: node3
    container_name: node3
    command: start --insecure --join=node1,node2,node3
    networks:
    - app-network

  haproxy:
```

```
      hostname: haproxy
      image: timveil/dynamic-haproxy:latest
      ports:
        - "26257:26257"
        - "8080:8080"
        - "8081:8081"
      environment:
        - NODES=node1 node2 node3
      links:
        - node1
        - node2
        - node3
      networks:
      - app-network

networks:
  app-network:
    driver: bridge
```

To start the containers running, initialize the cluster, and create a shell to one of the CockroachDB containers, run the following commands:

```
$ docker compose up -d
$ docker exec -it node1 cockroach init --insecure
$ docker exec -it node1 /bin/bash
```

Now that you're connected to the container, run the following command to connect to the CockroachDB SQL shell:

```
$ cockroach sql --insecure
```

You can now create the database and its objects exactly as you did before and access all of the nodes in the cluster via localhost:26257, a change that will be transparent to the running API.

Resilience Testing

Resilience testing aims to ensure that our database remains available in the event of node outages. We'll use the Docker Compose example that preceded this section as it's load balanced, meaning we can remove each node from the cluster one by one without having to connect to another. In our case, we have a three-node cluster, so it can tolerate up to a maximum of one unavailable node.

First, let's check that our nodes are running. We'll do this by running the `docker ps` command that only shows running containers and output their IDs and names:

```
$ docker ps --format '{{.ID}} {{.Names}}'
207279bf61f8 lb-haproxy-1
82b6ddd19251 node2
4552971fd61b node3
45759f6a0830 node1
```

Before we start removing nodes from the cluster, we'll check the range status of the cluster nodes. In the following output, I've kept only the relevant range information:

```
$ cockroach node status --ranges --insecure
 id | is_available | leaders | leaseholders | ranges | unavailable | underreplicated
-----+--------------+---------+--------------+--------+-------------+----------------
  1 | true         |    19   |     19       |  53    |     0       |        0
  2 | true         |    14   |     14       |  53    |     0       |        0
  3 | true         |    20   |     20       |  53    |     0       |        0
```

Let's remove one of the nodes from the cluster. We'll start by removing node1, seeing how cluster replication is affected, and then bring it back into the cluster before moving onto the next node:

```
$ docker stop 45759f6a0830
45759f6a0830
```

Stopping the Docker container in this way is equivalent to initiating a clean shutdown of a node; the node is drained before being terminated. This is fine for our purposes, as we're just asserting that the cluster continues running if one node goes away.

After a short pause, we'll rerun the `node status` command and see how this has affected the cluster:

```
$ cockroach node status --ranges --insecure
```

id	is_available	leaders	leaseholders	ranges	unavailable	underreplicated
1	false	0	0	53	0	0
2	true	22	22	53	0	22
3	true	31	31	53	0	31

We can see that node1 is now unavailable and has no leaseholders. Ranges in the remaining nodes now show as underreplicated because replication is no longer occurring over all three nodes. Let's bring node1 back up and see how this affects the replication:

```
$ docker start 45759f6a0830
45759f6a0830
```

```
$ cockroach node status --ranges --insecure
```

id	is_available	leaders	leaseholders	ranges	unavailable	underreplicated
1	true	13	13	53	0	0
2	true	18	18	53	0	0
3	true	24	24	53	0	0

We're back up to three nodes and our underreplication issue is resolved. I'll now repeat for node2. Note that I'm leaving a couple of minutes between stopping and starting a node before running the node status requests:

```
$ docker stop 82b6ddd19251
82b6ddd19251
```

```
$ cockroach node status --ranges --insecure
```

id	is_available	leaders	leaseholders	ranges	unavailable	underreplicated
1	true	22	22	53	0	22
2	true	0	0	53	0	0
3	true	31	31	53	0	31

```
$ docker start 82b6ddd19251
82b6ddd19251
```

```
$ cockroach node status --ranges --insecure
```

```
 id | is_available | leaders | leaseholders | ranges | unavailable | underreplicated
-----+--------------+---------+--------------+--------+-------------+----------------
  1 | true         |      17 |           17 |     53 |           0 |               0
  2 | true         |      13 |           13 |     53 |           0 |               0
  3 | true         |      23 |           23 |     53 |           0 |               0
```

Finally, we'll do the same for node3:

```
$ docker stop 4552971fd61b
4552971fd61b
```

```
$ cockroach node status --ranges --insecure
 id | is_available | leaders | leaseholders | ranges | unavailable | underreplicated
-----+--------------+---------+--------------+--------+-------------+----------------
  1 | true         |      28 |           28 |     53 |           0 |              28
  2 | true         |      25 |           25 |     53 |           0 |              25
  3 | true         |       0 |            0 |     53 |           0 |               0
```

```
$ docker start 4552971fd61b
4552971fd61b
```

```
$ cockroach node status --ranges --insecure
 id | is_available | leaders | leaseholders | ranges | unavailable | underreplicated
-----+--------------+---------+--------------+--------+-------------+----------------
  1 | true         |      22 |           22 |     53 |           0 |               0
  2 | true         |      18 |           18 |     53 |           0 |               0
  3 | true         |      13 |           13 |     53 |           0 |               0
```

Having finished our single-node shutdown tests, our server is back up to full capacity, having experienced no outages. Let's try removing two nodes from the cluster now:

```
$ docker stop 45759f6a0830 82b6ddd19251
45759f6a0830
82b6ddd19251
```

```
$ cockroach node status --ranges --insecure
ERROR: server closed the connection.
Is this a CockroachDB node?
```

```
EOF
Failed running "node status"
```

```
$ cockroach node status --ranges --insecure
```

id	is_available	leaders	leaseholders	ranges	unavailable	underreplicated
1	true	0	0	53	0	0
2	true	0	0	53	0	0
3	true	52	0	53	0	0

```
$ cockroach node status --ranges --insecure
```

id	is_available	leaders	leaseholders	ranges	unavailable	underreplicated
1	true	14	12	53	0	0
2	true	16	16	53	0	0
3	true	23	22	53	0	0

Observe that after we stopped two nodes, the cluster was no longer available. This is expected, because the maximum number of nodes we can tolerate being unavailable in a three-node cluster is one.

Also observe that after running the node status request immediately after restarting the nodes, none of them have any leaseholders. It's not until the restarted nodes (node1 and node2) become fully available that leaseholder leaders are reelected and the server returns to normal operation.

To finish our resilience tests, we'll clean things up:

```
$ docker compose down
[+] Running 5/5
 ⸬ Container lb-haproxy-1   Removed
 ⸬ Container node1          Removed
 ⸬ Container node2          Removed
 ⸬ Container node3          Removed
 ⸬ Network lb_app-network   Removed
```

CHAPTER 9

Production

In the last chapter of this book, we'll cover some practices and tools that will ensure our cluster is ready for whatever a production environment can throw at it:

- **Best practices** – Learning new technologies can be overwhelming, and knowing how to do things *correctly* can seem a daunting prospect. This section will explore some best practices to consider when running a production cluster.

- **Upgrading clusters** – We'll need to keep our nodes up to date to take advantage of the latest CockroachDB features and fixes.

- **Backing up and restoring data** – While CockroachDB's philosophy of being "multiactive" negates the need for DR (Disaster Recovery) planning, it's still good practice to consider taking database snapshots to return to in the event of accidental database corruption (e.g., `DELETE * FROM customer...`).

- **Moving a cluster** – Having had the privilege of working at the cosmetics retailer Lush, I appreciate that no cloud provider lasts forever.[1] This section will show you how to lift and shift a CockroachDB cluster from one place to another in the event of a major infrastructure overhaul.

---

[1] `https://cloud.google.com/customers/lush`

© Rob Reid 2022
R. Reid, *Practical CockroachDB*, https://doi.org/10.1007/978-1-4842-8224-3_9

Best Practices

The best practices documentation[2] on the Cockroach Labs website is comprehensive and a great reference for anyone wishing to get the best out of their CockroachDB clusters. We'll put these best practices to work in this section and see what happens if we don't.

Unless stated, many of the examples that follow in this chapter will use the three-node, load-balanced cluster I created in Chapter 8.

SELECT Performance

In this section, we'll look at some performance best practices concerning SELECT statements and what configuration values you can tweak to enjoy the best possible performance.

If you find that SELECT queries are running slowly and you've ruled out indexes as the culprit, your database might lack cache memory. By default, each node will have a cache size of 128MiB (~134MB), which stores information required by queries. This size works well as a default for local database development, but you may find that increasing it will make for faster SELECT performance. Cockroach Labs recommends setting the cache size to at least 25% of the machine's available memory for production deployments.

To update this setting, pass a value to the `--cache` argument when you start your node:

```
// Set the cache size to 30% of the node's total memory:
$ cockroach start --cache=.30 ...
$ cockroach start --cache=30% ...

// Set the cache size to a specific value:
$ cockroach start --cache=200MB ...
$ cockroach start --cache=200MiB ...
```

Another setting to consider changing is the `--max-sql-memory` argument, which will use 25% of a node's total memory by default. Increasing this value will allow CockroachDB to allocate more memory for aggregation operations like GROUP BY and ORDER BY and increase the number of possible concurrent connections to the database, easing connection pool contention.

---

[2] `www.cockroachlabs.com/docs/stable/performance-best-practices-overview`

To update this setting, pass a value to the `--max-sql-memory` argument when you start your node:

```
// Set the cache size to 30% of the node's total memory:
$ cockroach start --max-sql-memory=.30 ...
$ cockroach start --max-sql-memory=30% ...

// Set the cache size to a specific value:
$ cockroach start --max-sql-memory=200MB ...
$ cockroach start --max-sql-memory=200MiB ...
```

For a full list of memory recommendations, visit the flags section[3] of the start command documentation and the production checklist.[4]

INSERT Performance

In this section, we'll look at some performance best practices and why you'll want to follow them. We'll start by performing some INSERT statements to see why it's important to use multirow DML statements over single-row DML statements.

First, we'll create a database and a table:

```
CREATE TABLE sensor_reading (
    sensor_id UUID PRIMARY KEY,
    reading DECIMAL NOT NULL,
    timestamp TIMESTAMPTZ NOT NULL DEFAULT NOW()
);
```

Next, we'll write a script to simulate the bulk insertion of 1000 rows and compare the performance of doing it via single and multirow DML statements.

I'll use Go for these tests, so my imports and main function look as follows:

```
package main

import (
    "context"
    "fmt"
```

---

[3] www.cockroachlabs.com/docs/stable/cockroach-start#flags

[4] www.cockroachlabs.com/docs/stable/recommended-production-settings.html

```
        "log"
        "time"

        "github.com/google/uuid"
        "github.com/jackc/pgx/v4/pgxpool"
)

func main() {
        connStr := "postgres://root@localhost:26257/best_
        practices?sslmode=disable"
        db, err := pgxpool.Connect(context.Background(), connStr)
        if err != nil {
                log.Fatalf("error connecting to db: %v", err)
        }
        defer db.Close()

        ...

}
```

Next, we'll implement the single-row DML INSERT code. This code will make 1000 separate requests (involving 1000 separate network hops) to insert a row into the sensor_ reading table and time how long the complete operation takes:

```
func insertSingleRowDML(db *pgxpool.Pool, rows int) (time.Duration,
error) {
        const stmt = `INSERT INTO sensor_reading (sensor_id, reading) VALUES
($1, $2)`

        start := time.Now()
        for i := 0; i < rows; i++ {
                if _, err := db.Exec(context.Background(), stmt, uuid.New(),
                1); err != nil {
                        return 0, fmt.Errorf("inserting row: %w", err)
                }
        }
        return time.Since(start), nil
}
```

Next, we'll perform the single-row INSERT statements in batches. This will send multiple INSERT statements to CockroachDB at the same time and execute them in a single transaction. It's important to consider breaking large inserts into smaller ones when bulk-inserting data because the more data you're inserting, the longer you'll lock the table you're inserting into. The following function allows me to execute batch inserts in small, concurrent chunks:

```
func insertSingleRowDMLBatched(db *pgxpool.Pool, rows, chunks int) (time.
Duration, error) {
	const stmt = `INSERT INTO sensor_reading (sensor_id, reading) VALUES
	($1, $2)`

	start := time.Now()

	eg, _ := errgroup.WithContext(context.Background())
	for c := 0; c < chunks; c++ {
		eg.Go(func() error {
			batch := &pgx.Batch{}
			for i := 0; i < rows/chunks; i++ {
				batch.Queue(stmt, uuid.New(), i)
			}

			res := db.SendBatch(context.Background(), batch)
			if _, err := res.Exec(); err != nil {
				return fmt.Errorf("running batch query insert:
				%w", err)
			}

			return nil
		})
	}

	if err := eg.Wait(); err != nil {
		return 0, fmt.Errorf("in batch worker: %w", err)
	}

	return time.Since(start), nil
}
```

Note that this implementation is still executed as single-row DML in the database. The difference between this implementation and the first, however, is that there are now far fewer network hops, making for faster end-to-end queries.

If we really want to see performance gains from our queries, we'll need to execute multirow DML statements. The following does just that, with the help of two additional functions. The first helper function is called `counter`, and its job is to simply return an incremented number every time it's called:

```
func counter(start int) func() int {
    return func() int {
        defer func() { start++ }()
        return start
    }
}
```

The second helper function is called `argPlaceholders`, and its job is to manually construct the syntax used in a multirow DML statement.

```
func argPlaceholders(rows, columns, start int) string {
    builder := strings.Builder{}
    counter := counter(start)

    for r := 0; r < rows; r++ {
        builder.WriteString("(")
        for c := 0; c < columns; c++ {
            builder.WriteString("$")
            builder.WriteString(strconv.Itoa(counter()))

            if c < columns-1 {
                builder.WriteString(",")
            }
        }
        builder.WriteString(")")

        if r < rows-1 {
            builder.WriteString(",")
        }
```

```
        }

        return builder.String()
}
```

Here are some examples to help you understand how `argPlaceholders` works:

```
fmt.Println(argPlaceholders(1, 1, 1)) // -> ($1)
fmt.Println(argPlaceholders(1, 2, 1)) // -> ($1,$2)
fmt.Println(argPlaceholders(2, 1, 1)) // -> ($1),($2)
fmt.Println(argPlaceholders(3, 2, 1)) // -> ($1,$2),($3,$4),($5,$6)
```

Putting everything together, we get the multirow DML insert function:

```
func insertMultiRowDML(db *pgxpool.Pool, rows, chunks int) (time.Duration,
error) {
        const stmtFmt = `INSERT INTO sensor_reading (sensor_id, reading)
VALUES %s`

        start := time.Now()

        eg, _ := errgroup.WithContext(context.Background())
        for c := 0; c < chunks; c++ {
                eg.Go(func() error {
                        argPlaceholders := argPlaceholders(rows/chunks, 2, 1)
                        stmt := fmt.Sprintf(stmtFmt, argPlaceholders)

                        var args []interface{}
                        for i := 0; i < rows/chunks; i++ {
                                args = append(args, uuid.New(), i)
                        }

                        if _, err := db.Exec(context.Background(), stmt,
                        args...); err != nil {
                                return fmt.Errorf("inserting rows: %w", err)
                        }
                        return nil
                })
        }
```

```
if err := eg.Wait(); err != nil {
        return 0, fmt.Errorf("in batch worker: %w", err)
}

return time.Since(start), nil
}
```

So how fast are our queries? I'll run them each five times and take an average:

Test name	Duration
insertSingleRowDML (rows = 1000)	6.82s
insertSingleRowDMLBatched (rows = 1000, chunks = 1)	4.89s
insertSingleRowDMLBatched (rows = 1000, chunks = 2)	2.77s
insertSingleRowDMLBatched (rows = 1000, chunks = 4)	1.87s
insertMultiRowDMLBatched (rows = 1000, chunks = 1)	**49.35ms**
insertMultiRowDML (rows = 1000, chunks = 2)	**35.61ms**

It's clear to see that by executing multirow DML, our execution times are a fraction of the single-row DML equivalents. There's a good reason multirow DML statements for bulk operations are considered best practice.

UPDATE Performance

If you need to bulk update a table's data, it's important to consider the following:

- **Batching** – As with INSERT statements, large UPDATE statements will result in table locking and poor performance if not executed carefully. Run queries using multirow DML where possible.

- **Filtering** – Rather than attempting to update data on the fly, consider using a multipass technique, whereby the primary key columns for the rows needing updates are first selected before being used in a subsequent UPDATE statement. This way, CockroachDB is not being asked to run a slow, locking query but instead a nonlocking read query and then a fast, indexed locking query.

Let's compare the performance of an UPDATE statement that updates data on the fly vs. an UPDATE statement that uses the multipass approach. As with the INSERT examples, I'll provide code for both scenarios before running them.

Before we begin, we'll insert some random data into the table again, this time, shortcutting the Go code and going straight to CockroachDB with the help of its generate_series function. This statement will insert 1000 random entries into the table for the past 1000 or so days and will be the basis for our UPDATE statements:

```
INSERT INTO sensor_reading (sensor_id, reading, timestamp)
SELECT
    gen_random_uuid(),
    CAST(random() AS DECIMAL),
    '2022-02-18' - CAST(s * 10000 AS INTERVAL)
FROM generate_series(1, 100000) AS s;
```

Let's assume our sensor readings in the 1990s were high by 0.001 (no one said this wouldn't get hideously contrived) and need fixing. We'll fix the data using UPDATE statements.

First, we'll create update on-the-fly solution:

```
func updateOnTheFly(db *pgxpool.Pool) (time.Duration, error) {
    const stmt = `UPDATE sensor_reading
                    SET reading = reading - 0.001
                    WHERE date_trunc('decade', timestamp) = '1990-01-01'`

    start := time.Now()
    if _, err := db.Exec(context.Background(), stmt); err != nil {
        return 0, fmt.Errorf("updating rows: %w", err)
    }

    return time.Since(start), nil
}
```

Now, we'll create a multipass solution. There's more going on in this code than there was in the on-the-fly example, simply because we're performing more operations to achieve a faster query that results in less index contention. For this example, I present three functions.

First, a function to select IDs out of the table (note that you can select whatever column(s) will allow you to most efficiently fetch your data). This function

- Creates a SQL statement and injects an additional selection criterion if we've already run an iteration and collected an offset ID from which to begin the next batch of IDs to update[5]

- Selects the IDs of any rows matching the selection criteria using a time-travel[6] query (a query that tolerates slightly stale data in return for reduced transaction contention and increased performance)

- Creates an array of IDs to return

We'll name the function updateMultiPassSelect:

```go
func updateMultiPassSelect(db *pgxpool.Pool, lastID string, selectLimit
int) ([]string, error) {
    const selectStmtFmt = `SELECT sensor_id FROM sensor_reading
                           AS OF SYSTEM TIME '-5s'
                           WHERE date_trunc('decade', timestamp) =
                           '1990-01-01'
                           %s
                           ORDER BY sensor_id
                           LIMIT $1`

    args := []interface{}{}

    selectStmt := selectStmtFmt
    if lastID != "" {
        selectStmt = fmt.Sprintf(selectStmtFmt, "AND sensor_id > $2")
        args = append(args, selectLimit, lastID)
    } else {
```

---

[5] This is frequently referred to as "cursor pagination."
[6] www.cockroachlabs.com/docs/stable/as-of-system-time.html

216

```
            selectStmt = fmt.Sprintf(selectStmtFmt, "")
            args = append(args, selectLimit)
    }

    // Fetch ids in a batch.
    rows, err := db.Query(context.Background(), selectStmt, args...)
    if err != nil {
            return nil, fmt.Errorf("fetching rows: %w", err)
    }

    // Read the ids into a collection.
    ids := []string{}
    var id string
    for rows.Next() {
            if err = rows.Scan(&id); err != nil {
                    return nil, fmt.Errorf("scanning row: %w", err)
            }
            ids = append(ids, id)
    }

    return ids, nil
}
```

The next function will update any rows matching the IDs we fetched from the previous query. This function

- Creates a subset of the IDs passed

- Runs a query to update rows based on that ID subset

- Updates the ID subset to point to a different set of IDs

- Once all IDs have been processed, returns

We'll name the function updateMultiPassUpdate:

```
func updateMultiPassUpdate(db *pgxpool.Pool, ids []string, limit
int) error {
    const updateStmt = `UPDATE sensor_reading
                        SET reading = reading - 0.001
                        WHERE sensor_id = ANY $1`
```

```
        updateIDs := ids
        for {
                idCount := min(len(updateIDs), limit)
                if idCount == 0 {
                    return nil
                }

                if _, err := db.Exec(context.Background(), updateStmt,
                pq.Array(updateIDs[:idCount])); err != nil {
                        return fmt.Errorf("updating rows: %w", err)
                }

                if idCount < limit {
                    return nil
                }

                updateIDs = updateIDs[idCount:]
        }
}

func min(x, y int) int {
    if x < y {
        return x
    }
    return y
}
```

And finally, the function itself. This

- Fetches a batch of IDs that have not been processed via the select function and passes them to the update function.

- If at any point we've run out of IDs to process, the function returns.

We'll name this function updateMultiPass:

```
func updateMultiPass(db *pgxpool.Pool, selectLimit, updateLimit int) (d
time.Duration, err error) {
    start := time.Now()
    var lastID string
```

```
for {
        ids, err := updateMultiPassSelect(db, lastID, selectLimit)
        if err != nil {
                return 0, fmt.Errorf("fetching ids to update: %w", err)
        }

        if len(ids) == 0 {
                break
        }

        if err = updateMultiPassUpdate(db, ids, updateLimit); err
        != nil {
                return 0, fmt.Errorf("updating items: %w", err)
        }

        if len(ids) < 1000 {
                break
        }

        lastID = ids[len(ids)-1]
    }

    return time.Since(start), nil
}
```

Now for the results. The difference between the two methods isn't as obvious as the INSERT example, but for the reduced table locking, an additional performance bump is great:

Test name	Duration
updateOnTheFly	3.69s
updateMultiPass (selectLimit = 10,000, updateLimit = 1,000)	**2.04s**

Check out the Cockroach Labs site for a great example of a multipass bulk-update operation using Python.[7]

---

[7]www.cockroachlabs.com/docs/stable/bulk-update-data

Cluster Maintenance

The cluster you originally deploy to production on day one is unlikely to resemble the cluster you have running after year one (and especially after year five). If you're planning your CockroachDB cluster years ahead, you

- Are potentially paying for resources you're not making full use of

- Are not taking full advantage of CockroachDB's scaling capabilities

In this section, we'll create a small cluster of nodes and perform the following cluster-wide operations:

- Scale the cluster by adding additional nodes.

- Increment the version of CockroachDB.

- Move the cluster onto new nodes.

We'll start with scaling the cluster. If your CockroachDB deployment is running via Cockroach Cloud, this scenario is handled for you; all cluster scaling is automatic. If your cluster is hosted in Kubernetes, it's as simple as follows:

```
apiVersion: apps/v1
kind: StatefulSet
metadata:
  name: cockroachdb
spec:
  serviceName: "cockroachdb"
  replicas: 3 # => 5
  ...
```

For the examples in this chapter, we'll spin up a cluster manually, so we have full control over each of the nodes. Let's start with three nodes in three separate command-line terminal sessions and then initialize it with a fourth terminal. Note that I'm using different ports and stores in this example because the cluster is running on one machine. In reality, this cluster will be running across multiple machines, so the only difference between the node start command will be the join addresses:

```
$ cockroach start \
  --insecure \
  --store=node1 \
```

```
  --listen-addr=localhost:26257 \
  --http-addr=localhost:8080 \
  --join=localhost:26257,localhost:26258,localhost:26259

$ cockroach start \
  --insecure \
  --store=node2 \
  --listen-addr=localhost:26258 \
  --http-addr=localhost:8081 \
  --join=localhost:26257,localhost:26258,localhost:26259

$ cockroach start \
  --insecure \
  --store=node3 \
  --listen-addr=localhost:26259 \
  --http-addr=localhost:8082 \
  --join=localhost:26257,localhost:26258,localhost:26259

$ cockroach init --insecure --host=localhost:26257
```

Time to scale it. CockroachDB was designed to run anywhere, with scalability and survivability being its raison d'etre. As such, scaling a CockroachDB cluster is almost comically simple:

```
$ cockroach start \
  --insecure \
  --store=node4 \
  --listen-addr=localhost:26260 \
  --http-addr=localhost:8083 \
  --join=localhost:26257,localhost:26258,localhost:26259
```

In the preceding command, we start a new node in the exact same way we started the three initial (or "seed") nodes. Every node in the cluster will use the gossip protocol[8] to communicate with one other to organize scaling. The three seed nodes are all it takes

---

[8] https://en.wikipedia.org/wiki/Gossip_protocol

to create the basis for this gossip network, and they don't need to be aware of additional nodes. This allows you to continue to scale your cluster without making any changes to the configuration of the seed nodes.

Running the command starts a fourth node, which immediately joins the cluster, expanding its capacity.

Before moving onto the next example, stop the nodes and remove their data directories (e.g., node1, node2, and node3).

Scaling a cluster into a different region requires a little more configuration but is about as straightforward as scaling a single-region cluster. First, we'll create a cluster in eu-central-1 (Frankfurt) before scaling into eu-west-3 (Paris):

```
$ cockroach start \
  --insecure \
  --store=node1 \
  --listen-addr=localhost:26257 \
  --http-addr=localhost:8080 \
  --locality=region=eu-central-1,zone=eu-central-1a \
  --join='localhost:26257, localhost:26258, localhost:26259'

$ cockroach start \
  --insecure \
  --store=node2 \
  --listen-addr=localhost:26258 \
  --http-addr=localhost:8081 \
  --locality=region=eu-central-1,zone=eu-central-1a \
  --join='localhost:26257, localhost:26258, localhost:26259'

$ cockroach start \
  --insecure \
  --store=node3 \
  --listen-addr=localhost:26259 \
  --http-addr=localhost:8082 \
  --locality=region=eu-central-1,zone=eu-central-1a \
  --join='localhost:26257, localhost:26258, localhost:26259'

$ cockroach init --insecure --host=localhost:26257
```

With the nodes in Frankfurt up and running, let's use the CockroachDB shell to interrogate the regions and zones:

```
$ cockroach sql --insecure

SHOW regions;
     region    |      zones       | database_names | primary_region_of
---------------+------------------+----------------+--------------------
  eu-central-1 | {eu-central-1a}  | {}             | {}
```

Now, we'll spin up the nodes in our Paris cluster and have them join the nodes in the existing Frankfurt cluster:

```
$ cockroach start \
  --insecure \
  --store=node4 \
  --listen-addr=localhost:26260 \
  --http-addr=localhost:8083 \
  --locality=region=eu-west-3,zone=eu-west-3a \
  --join='localhost:26257, localhost:26258, localhost:26259'

$ cockroach start \
  --insecure \
  --store=node5 \
  --listen-addr=localhost:26261 \
  --http-addr=localhost:8084 \
  --locality=region=eu-west-3,zone=eu-west-3a \
  --join='localhost:26257, localhost:26258, localhost:26259'

$ cockroach start \
  --insecure \
  --store=node6 \
  --listen-addr=localhost:26262 \
  --http-addr=localhost:8085 \
  --locality=region=eu-west-3,zone=eu-west-3a \
  --join='localhost:26257, localhost:26258, localhost:26259'
```

With the nodes in Paris up and running, let's run the regions query again to see how our cluster looks now:

```
SHOW regions;
     region     |       zones      | database_names | primary_region_of
----------------+------------------+----------------+--------------------
  eu-central-1  | {eu-central-1a}  | {}             | {}
  eu-west-3     | {eu-west-3a}     | {}             | {}
```

Next, we'll upgrade the version of CockroachDB on all of our cluster nodes. Starting with just the nodes of the Frankfurt cluster for simplicity, we'll update each of the nodes in turn, with zero downtime.

On my machine, the Frankfurt nodes are currently running on v21.2.0 of CockroachDB:

```
$ cockroach version
Build Tag:        v21.2.0
Build Time:       2021/11/15 14:00:58
Distribution:     CCL
Platform:         darwin amd64 (x86_64-apple-darwin19)
Go Version:       go1.16.6
C Compiler:       Clang 10.0.0
Build Commit ID:  79e5979416cb426092a83beff0be1c20aebf84c6
Build Type:       release
```

The most up-to-date version of CockroachDB available at the time of writing is v21.2.5. Following an upgrade of CockroachDB, I can confirm this on the command line:

```
$ cockroach version
Build Tag:        v21.2.5
Build Time:       2022/02/07 21:04:05
Distribution:     CCL
Platform:         darwin amd64 (x86_64-apple-darwin19)
Go Version:       go1.16.6
C Compiler:       Clang 10.0.0
Build Commit ID:  5afb632f77eee9f09f2adfa2943e1979ec4ebedf
Build Type:       release
```

Let's apply this version of CockroachDB to each of the nodes. In an environment where you've manually configured load balancing, you'll need to remove nodes from the load balancer before removing them from the cluster. This will prevent any requests from being routed to a dead node. For Kubernetes users, the following is safe to do:

```
apiVersion: apps/v1
kind: StatefulSet

...

    containers:
    - name: cockroachdb
      image: cockroachdb/cockroach:v21.2.0 # => cockroachdb/cockroach:v21.2.5
      imagePullPolicy: IfNotPresent
```

Kubernetes will perform a rolling upgrade of your nodes, without any downtime, and will remove each node from the load balancer before replacing it.

Cockroach Labs has some best practices[9] to consider when performing an upgrade between versions (including minor versions like the update we're about to do). A key thing to be aware of is auto-finalization and whether it's enabled or not before you upgrade your nodes.

If there's any chance that by upgrading your cluster nodes you could inadvertently corrupt your database (e.g., when upgrading between versions with breaking changes), it's important to disable auto-finalization. This can be achieved as follows:

```
SET CLUSTER SETTING cluster.preserve_downgrade_option = '21.2';
```

And to reenable auto-finalization:

```
RESET CLUSTER SETTING cluster.preserve_downgrade_option;
```

Before we begin, I'll run a statement from a previous chapter to get basic information about the nodes in the cluster:

```
$ cockroach node status --insecure
  id |     address      |   sql_address    |  build  |
-----+------------------+------------------+---------+
   1 | localhost:26257  | localhost:26257  | v21.2.0 |
   2 | localhost:26258  | localhost:26258  | v21.2.0 |
   3 | localhost:26259  | localhost:26259  | v21.2.0 |
```

---

[9]www.cockroachlabs.com/docs/stable/upgrade-cockroach-version.html

As we can see, all of our nodes are running v21.2.0 as expected. Let's perform our rolling upgrade now, starting with node one. First, we'll stop the node (just `ctrl-c` the process for now) and check that it has become unavailable. Note that we'll have to connect to another node to check the status while node one is down:

```
$ cockroach node status --insecure --url postgres://localhost:26258
id |     address      |   sql_address    |  build  | is_available | is_live
---+------------------+------------------+---------+--------------+----------
1  | localhost:26257  | localhost:26257  | v21.2.0 | false        | false
2  | localhost:26258  | localhost:26258  | v21.2.0 | true         | true
3  | localhost:26259  | localhost:26259  | v21.2.0 | true         | true
```

As there are no breaking changes between v21.2.0 and v21.2.5, we can simply run the start command again once we've obtained v21.2.5 of the binary; we don't need to delete the node's store directory.

Starting the node again, we can see that the node is available again and its version has incremented. We can also run the node command against node one again:

```
$ cockroach node status --insecure
  id |     address      |   sql_address    |  build  |
-----+------------------+------------------+---------+
  1  | localhost:26257  | localhost:26257  | v21.2.5 |
  2  | localhost:26258  | localhost:26258  | v21.2.0 |
  3  | localhost:26259  | localhost:26259  | v21.2.0 |
```

We'll repeat the steps for nodes two and three now. Note that because our cluster has only three nodes, it's critical that we perform the upgrade on one node at a time. If we remove two nodes from the cluster at the same time, the cluster will be unavailable.

```
$ cockroach node status --insecure
  id |     address      |   sql_address    |  build  |
-----+------------------+------------------+---------+
  1  | localhost:26257  | localhost:26257  | v21.2.5 |
  2  | localhost:26258  | localhost:26258  | v21.2.5 |
  3  | localhost:26259  | localhost:26259  | v21.2.5 |
```

Moving a Cluster

Let's assume that in the last part of this section, we need to move a cluster from one location to another (e.g., for a cloud provider migration or simply onto newer hardware in an on-premise scenario). I won't discuss topics like load balancing or DNS here but provide a pattern for the migration of nodes.

We'll start a brand new cluster for this example, starting with a three-node cluster in AWS's eu-central-1 (Frankfurt) region and moving them into GCP's europe-west1 (St. Ghislain) region. Everything will be running locally, so note that no cloud migration is actually taking place.

Before we begin, it's important to discuss the order in which we'll add and remove nodes. We have a three-node cluster, with a replication factor of three (as can be seen by running SHOW ZONE CONFIGURATION FROM DATABASE defaultdb), so we should keep a three-node cluster available at all times. This means bringing up a node before taking another node down and waiting for all replicas to be rebalanced onto the new node before starting work on the next node.

First, we'll start node1, node2, and node3 in the Frankfurt region and initialize the cluster:

```
$ cockroach start \
  --insecure \
  --store=node1 \
  --listen-addr=localhost:26257 \
  --http-addr=localhost:8080 \
  --locality=region=eu-central-1,zone=eu-central-1a \
  --join='localhost:26257, localhost:26258, localhost:26259'

$ cockroach start \
  --insecure \
  --store=node2 \
  --listen-addr=localhost:26258 \
  --http-addr=localhost:8081 \
  --locality=region=eu-central-1,zone=eu-central-1a \
  --join='localhost:26257, localhost:26258, localhost:26259'

$ cockroach start \
  --insecure \
  --store=node3 \
```

```
--listen-addr=localhost:26259 \
--http-addr=localhost:8082 \
--locality=region=eu-central-1,zone=eu-central-1a \
--join='localhost:26257, localhost:26258, localhost:26259'
```

```
$ cockroach init --insecure --host=localhost:26257
```

Next, we'll start node4, node5, and node6 in the St. Ghislain region and have them join the cluster. Once any underreplicated ranges have been rebalanced and resolved, we'll start tearing down the original cluster nodes:

```
$ cockroach start \
  --insecure \
  --store=node4 \
  --listen-addr=localhost:26260 \
  --http-addr=localhost:8083 \
  --locality=region=europe-west1,zone=europe-west1b \
  --join='localhost:26257, localhost:26258, localhost:26259,
localhost:26260, localhost:26261, localhost:26262'
```

```
$ cockroach start \
  --insecure \
  --store=node5 \
  --listen-addr=localhost:26261 \
  --http-addr=localhost:8084 \
  --locality=region=europe-west1,zone=europe-west1c \
  --join='localhost:26257, localhost:26258, localhost:26259,
localhost:26260, localhost:26261, localhost:26262'
```

```
$ cockroach start \
  --insecure \
  --store=node6 \
  --listen-addr=localhost:26262 \
  --http-addr=localhost:8085 \
  --locality=region=europe-west1,zone=europe-west1d \
  --join='localhost:26257, localhost:26258, localhost:26259,
    localhost:26260, localhost:26261, localhost:26262'
```

Note that I've included all of the new and existing hosts to the `--join` argument; this will prevent the cluster from becoming unavailable once I start removing the old nodes.

With the new nodes in place and all underreplicated ranges resolved, let's run the node command to see how our cluster is looking:

```
$ cockroach node status --insecure --url postgres://localhost:26260
--format records

-[ RECORD 1 ]
id           | 1
address      | localhost:26257
locality     | region=eu-central-1,zone=eu-central-1a
is_available | true
is_live      | true

-[ RECORD 2 ]
id           | 2
address      | localhost:26259
locality     | region=eu-central-1,zone=eu-central-1a
is_available | true
is_live      | true

-[ RECORD 3 ]
id           | 3
address      | localhost:26258
locality     | region=eu-central-1,zone=eu-central-1a
is_available | true
is_live      | true

-[ RECORD 4 ]
id           | 4
address      | localhost:26260
locality     | region=europe-west1,zone=europe-west1b
is_available | true
is_live      | true
```

```
-[ RECORD 5 ]
id           | 5
address      | localhost:26261
locality     | region=europe-west1,zone=europe-west1c
is_available | true
is_live      | true

-[ RECORD 6 ]
id           | 6
address      | localhost:26262
locality     | region=europe-west1,zone=europe-west1d
is_available | true
is_live      | true
```

Everything's looking good. All six nodes are operational. Once all remaining underreplicated ranges are resolved (see Figure 9-1 for an example of healthy replication) and you've taken any backups required, it's safe to remove the original three nodes from the cluster and finish the move.

Node Status			Replication Status		
6	0	0	43	0	0
				UNDER-	
LIVE	SUSPECT	DEAD	TOTAL	REPLICATED	UNAVAILABLE
NODES	NODES	NODES	RANGES	RANGES	RANGES

Figure 9-1. *Replication status of six healthy nodes*

Let's start by decommissioning node1, node2, and node3. This process will ensure that all ranges are replicated away from these nodes and then remove them from the cluster. Note that I'm connected to node6 but I could have connected to any node in the cluster to perform this operation:

```
$ cockroach node decommission 1 --insecure --url postgres://localhost:26262
$ cockroach node decommission 2 --insecure --url postgres://localhost:26262
$ cockroach node decommission 3 --insecure --url postgres://localhost:26262
```

Once the nodes are decommissioned, check that the replication status in the dashboard still looks like Figure 9-1 and then shut the nodes down.

You've just moved your cluster from AWS's Frankfurt region to GCP's St. Ghislain region!

Backing Up and Restoring Data

Being a multiactive database, CockroachDB does not require the conventional DR (Disaster Recovery) architecture of many traditional relational databases. Unfortunately, a multiactive database will not protect you against bad actors or simply bad mistakes; a TRUNCATE statement may wreak as much havoc on a CockroachDB as any other relational database.

That's where backups come to the rescue. With CockroachDB, you can back up your clusters in any of the following ways:[10]

- **Full backups** – Full backups contain all of the data in your cluster (without replication). Say, for example, you replicate 1GB of data across five nodes; your backup will contain 1GB of data, not 5GB. Full backups are available for all clusters.

- **Incremental backups** – Incremental backups capture the changes since the last backup was made. You'll always need at least one full backup but can take as many incremental backups as you like. Incremental backups are available for Enterprise clusters.

- **Encrypted backups** – Encrypted backups add an additional level of security to your database backups. Note that you can achieve secure backups without manual encryption by simply backing up into an encrypted S3 bucket (or similar). Encrypted backups are available for Enterprise clusters.

- **Backups with revision history** – Backups with revision history not only back up the latest data in the database but also any revision history yet to be garbage collected (you'll have 25 hours' worth of revision history by default). From these backups, you can restore

---

[10] www.cockroachlabs.com/docs/v21.2/take-full-and-incremental-backups

either the latest data or data from a previous point in time. These are available for Enterprise clusters.

- **Locality-aware backups** – Locality-aware backups allow specific database localities (e.g., just eu-central-1) to be backed up and are available for Enterprise clusters.

Let's run through each of the backup methods to see how they work for different use cases. I'll run each of the following examples in a demo cluster (which enables Enterprise features). To enable Enterprise features in a regular cluster, configure the following settings:

```
$ cockroach sql --insecure --host=<YOUR_HOST>
$ SET CLUSTER SETTING cluster.organization = 'your_organisation';
$ SET CLUSTER SETTING enterprise.license = 'your_license_key';
```

Before we create any backups, I'll create a small database and table to prove that our backup and restore operations are successful. For this, I'll create a *new* sensor_reading table that will work nicely for all of the backup methods:

```
CREATE TABLE sensor_reading (
    sensor_id UUID PRIMARY KEY,
    country STRING NOT NULL,
    reading DECIMAL NOT NULL,
    timestamp TIMESTAMPTZ NOT NULL DEFAULT NOW()
);

INSERT INTO sensor_reading (sensor_id, country, reading, timestamp)
SELECT
    gen_random_uuid(),
    'DE',
    CAST(random() AS DECIMAL),
    '2022-02-18' - CAST(s * 10000 AS INTERVAL)
FROM generate_series(1, 1000) AS s;
```

Just one more step before we're ready to backup. Unlike the IMPORT statement, which can use an HTTP endpoint, backups and restorations need to use cloud provider blob storage (e.g., S3, Google Cloud Storage, and Azure Storage). Let's create a few S3 buckets for our backup examples:

```
$ aws s3api create-bucket \
    --bucket practical-cockroachdb-backups \
    --region eu-west-2 \
    --create-bucket-configuration LocationConstraint=eu-west-2

{
    "Location": "http://practical-cockroachdb-backups.s3.amazonaws.com/"
}

$ aws s3api create-bucket \
    --bucket practical-cockroachdb-backups-us-west \
    --region us-west-1 \
    --create-bucket-configuration LocationConstraint=us-west-1

{
    "Location": "http://practical-cockroachdb-backups-us-west.
s3.amazonaws.com/"
}

$ aws s3api create-bucket \
    --bucket practical-cockroachdb-backups-us-east \
    --region us-east-1

{
    "Location": "/practical-cockroachdb-backups-us-east"
}
```

Full Backups

With the database, table, and bucket in place, we're ready to begin! Let's start by running a full backup and restore of the data:

```
BACKUP INTO 's3://practical-cockroachdb-backups?AWS_ACCESS_KEY_ID=****&AWS_
SECRET_ACCESS_KEY=****&AWS_REGION=eu-west-2' AS OF SYSTEM TIME '-10s';
        job_id       |  status   | fraction_completed | rows | index_entries | bytes
---------------------+-----------+--------------------+------+---------------+------
 742270852339073025  | succeeded |                  1 | 1032 |            20 | 57311
```

Note that in our backup request, we tell CockroachDB to back up the database as it was ten seconds ago. This means that it's not trying to back up live data while it's being served to clients. This is a performance recommendation from Cockroach Labs, and ten seconds is the *minimum* recommended period; depending on your garbage collection window (the default is 25 hours), you may want to set this to be further in the past.

Let's check that S3 has our backup:

```
$ aws s3api list-objects-v2 \
    --bucket practical-cockroachdb-backups

{
    "Contents": [
        {
            "Key": "2022/03/06-190437.13/BACKUP-
            CHECKPOINT-742270852339073025-CHECKSUM",
            "LastModified": "2022-03-06T19:04:48+00:00",
            "ETag": "\"79f98a6fd4b39f02b7727c91707b71cd\"",
            "Size": 4,
            "StorageClass": "STANDARD"
        }
        ...
```

Looks good! CockroachDB backups are stored in a directory structure whose directories indicate the date and time of the backup.

Let's ensure our sensor_reading table was backed up successfully by running a restore. As all of the data is safely replicated across our three nodes, a restore won't currently prove anything; let's remedy that:

```
TRUNCATE sensor_reading;

SELECT COUNT(*) FROM sensor_reading;
  count
---------
      0
```

With the data gone (and the department panicking), it's time to run our restore. Pay attention to the backups objects' directory structure, we'll need them now:

```
RESTORE FROM '2022/03/06-190437.13' IN 's3://practical-cockroachdb-
backups?AWS_ACCESS_KEY_ID=****&AWS_SECRET_ACCESS_KEY=****&AWS_
REGION=eu-west-2';
```

```
ERROR: full cluster restore can only be run on a cluster with no tables or
databases but found 4 descriptors: [sensors crdb_internal_region _crdb_
internal_region sensor_reading]
```

Oh no! It seems we can't restore unless we have an empty cluster. What if we had other databases or tables that are not in need of restoration? Happily, CockroachDB has alternative RESTORE commands you can use, depending on your situation. All of which can be performed from the full backup we just took:

- **Ruined your cluster?** – Use RESTORE FROM to restore your entire cluster.

- **Ruined your database?** – Use RESTORE DATABASE {DATABASE} FROM to restore just your database.

- **Ruined your table?** – Use RESTORE TABLE {DATABASE}.{TABLE} FROM to restore just your table. Note that by passing in a comma-separated string of tables, you can back up multiple tables in one go.

There's one more step we need to perform before our table can be restored. We need to DROP or RENAME it[11] before running the restore. As my sensor_reading table is empty, there's nothing I need to archive, so DROP works best for me:

```
DROP TABLE sensor_reading;
```

```
RESTORE TABLE sensors.sensor_reading FROM '2022/03/06-190437.13' IN 's3://
practical-cockroachdb-backups?AWS_ACCESS_KEY_ID=****&AWS_SECRET_ACCESS_
KEY=****&AWS_REGION=eu-west-2';
```

---

[11] www.cockroachlabs.com/docs/stable/restore.html#restore-a-cluster

job_id	status	fraction_completed	rows	index_entries	bytes
742274102397501441	succeeded	1	1000	0	52134

Incremental Backups

A full backup and restore works in this case, as the database and objects are small. If your cluster is many gigabytes in size, incremental backups may be a more efficient option for you. Let's explore incremental backups to see how they work.

First, we'll insert some new data into our restored sensor_reading table to simulate data being added to the table over time. This will create a delta between the original data we inserted at the start of the backups section to now. If CockroachDB does not detect a change between an incremental backup and the previous backup (whether full or incremental), you'll see an empty backup directory:

```
INSERT INTO sensor_reading (sensor_id, country, reading, timestamp)
SELECT
    gen_random_uuid(),
    'DE',
    CAST(random() AS DECIMAL),
    '2022-02-18' - CAST(s * 10000 AS INTERVAL)
FROM generate_series(1, 500) AS s;

SELECT COUNT(*) FROM sensor_reading;
  count
---------
   1500
```

Now, let's run an incremental backup:

```
BACKUP INTO LATEST IN 's3://practical-cockroachdb-backups?AWS_ACCESS_KEY_
ID=****&AWS_SECRET_ACCESS_KEY=****&AWS_REGION=eu-west-2' AS OF SYSTEM
TIME '-10s';
```

job_id	status	fraction_completed	rows	index_entries	bytes
742278826975625217	succeeded	1	1511	35	85097

The number of rows indicates the number of rows backed up by the last backup operation. Note that because we have not yet backed up our restored dataset, the delta includes all rows in the table. If you run again now, you'll see zero rows as there's nothing fresh to back up:

```
BACKUP INTO LATEST IN 's3://practical-cockroachdb-backups?AWS_ACCESS_KEY_
ID=****&AWS_SECRET_ACCESS_KEY=****&AWS_REGION=eu-west-2' AS OF SYSTEM
TIME '-10s';
```

job_id	status	fraction_completed	rows	index_entries	bytes
742280265162588161	succeeded	1	0	0	0

Note that because we're running an incremental backup of the whole cluster, changes to any other database object will be picked up (and backed up). To restore our table, we simply need to rerun the restore operation as before. All incremental backups exist in S3 and are automatically picked up:

```
RESTORE TABLE sensors.sensor_reading FROM '2022/03/06-190437.13' IN 's3://
practical-cockroachdb-backups?AWS_ACCESS_KEY_ID=****&AWS_SECRET_ACCESS_
KEY=****&AWS_REGION=eu-west-2';
```

Encrypted Backups

To encrypt a backup, you'll need to create your own encryption key and use that to encrypt the backup before it's persisted in cloud storage. Let's create an encryption key and use it to create an encrypted backup now:

```
$ aws kms create-key \
    --key-spec=SYMMETRIC_DEFAULT \
    --tags TagKey=Purpose,TagValue="Encrypt CockroachDB backups" \
    --description "Practical CockroachDB Backups"
```

To use the encryption key for backups and restores, simply pass an argument to the BACKUP/RESTORE command as follows:

```
BACKUP INTO 's3://practical-cockroachdb-backups?AWS_ACCESS_KEY_ID=****&AWS_
SECRET_ACCESS_KEY=****&AWS_REGION=eu-west-2'
    WITH kms = 'aws:///****?AUTH=implicit&REGION=eu-west-2';
```

There are a few things to note here:

- The KMS key URL scheme of "aws:///" is not a typo.

- The key ID to use in the URL can be obtained by running the following AWS CLI command and extracting the KeyId for the key you'd like to use:

```
$ aws kms list-keys
{
  "Keys": [
    {
      "KeyId": "********-****-****-****-***********",
      "KeyArn": "arn:aws:kms:eu-west-2:***:key/********-****-****-****-
      ***********"
    },
    {
      "KeyId": "********-****-****-****-***********",
      "KeyArn": "arn:aws:kms:eu-west-2:***:key/********-****-****-****-
      ***********"
    }
  ]
}
```

- By using the configuration AUTH=implicit, I'm telling CockroachDB to use the same credentials to access the KMS key as it used to access the bucket. If your KMS key uses different credentials, provide the associated AWS_ACCESS_KEY_ID, AWS_SECRET_ACCESS_KEY, and REGION query arguments for that key.

If you attempt to restore the backup without a KMS key, you'll receive an error, as CockroachDB is aware that this backup has been manually encrypted with a KMS key:

```
RESTORE TABLE sensors.sensor_reading FROM '2022/03/08-183653.00' IN 's3://
practical-cockroachdb-backups?AWS_ACCESS_KEY_ID=****&AWS_SECRET_ACCESS_
KEY=****&AWS_REGION=eu-west-2';
```

ERROR: file appears encrypted -- *try specifying one of "encryption_
passphrase" or "kms": proto: wrong wireType = 5 for field EntryCounts*

Restoring from a backup *with* the use of a KMS key performs the restore as expected:

```
RESTORE TABLE sensors.sensor_reading FROM '2022/03/08-183653.00' IN 's3://
practical-cockroachdb-backups?AWS_ACCESS_KEY_ID=****&AWS_SECRET_ACCESS_
KEY=****&AWS_REGION=eu-west-2'
  WITH kms = 'aws:///****?AUTH=implicit&REGION=eu-west-2';
```

job_id	status	fraction_completed	rows	index_entries	bytes
742834697875423233	succeeded	1	1000	0	52140

To encrypt a multiregion cluster using KMS keys stored in different regions, simply provide a KMS key for each of the regions you'd like to encrypt. The cluster I'm encrypting is currently in a single region, but by adding more KMS keys to the array of keys, you can encrypt more regions:

```
BACKUP INTO 's3://practical-cockroachdb-backups?AWS_ACCESS_KEY_ID=****&AWS_
SECRET_ACCESS_KEY=****&AWS_REGION=eu-west-2'
  WITH kms = (
    'aws:///****AUTH=implicit&REGION=eu-west-2'
  );
```

job_id	status	fraction_completed	rows	index_entries	bytes
742839873407320065	succeeded	1	1055	65	76388

```
RESTORE TABLE sensors.sensor_reading FROM '2022/03/08-191858.46' IN 's3://
practical-cockroachdb-backups?AWS_ACCESS_KEY_ID=****&AWS_SECRET_ACCESS_
KEY=****&AWS_REGION=eu-west-2'
  WITH kms = (
    'aws:///****AUTH=implicit&REGION=eu-west-2'
  );
```

job_id	status	fraction_completed	rows	index_entries	bytes
742840069222793217	succeeded	1	1000	0	52150

Note that the number of rows restored is less than the number of rows backed up. This is because a backup was made across the whole cluster, while the restore targets just the sensor_reading table.

If you'd rather not use keys stored in your cloud provider for encrypting backups, you can provide your own password to use for encryption. The process of encrypting backups in this manner is very similar to encrypt backups with cloud keys:

```
BACKUP INTO 's3://practical-cockroachdb-backups?AWS_ACCESS_KEY_ID=****&AWS_
SECRET_ACCESS_KEY=****&AWS_REGION=eu-west-2'
  WITH encryption_passphrase = 'correct horse battery staple';
```

job_id	status	fraction_completed	rows	index_entries	bytes
742837673818750977	succeeded	1	1046	48	69464

The restore is also very similar to the KMS equivalent:

```
RESTORE TABLE sensors.sensor_reading FROM '2022/03/08-190747.27' IN 's3://
practical-cockroachdb-backups?AWS_ACCESS_KEY_ID=****&AWS_SECRET_ACCESS_
KEY=****&AWS_REGION=eu-west-2'
  WITH encryption_passphrase = 'correct horse battery staple';
```

job_id	status	fraction_completed	rows	index_entries	bytes
742838121558212609	succeeded	1	1000	0	52150

Locality-Aware Backups

To make a backup locality-aware, we simply need to pass some additional configuration to the BACKUP command to make sure that backups remain in their respective regions. Let's create a new cluster using the demo command to simulate a multiregion cluster.

In the following example, we specify that by default, CockroachDB should back up to the us-west bucket, except for nodes with the us-east-1 locality, which will back up to the us-east bucket:

```
BACKUP INTO (
's3://practical-cockroachdb-backups-us-west?AWS_ACCESS_KEY_ID=****&AWS_
SECRET_ACCESS_KEY=****&COCKROACH_LOCALITY=default',
```

```
's3://practical-cockroachdb-backups-us-east?AWS_ACCESS_KEY_ID=****&AWS_
SECRET_ACCESS_KEY=****&COCKROACH_LOCALITY=region%3Dus-east-1'
);

RESTORE TABLE sensor_reading FROM '2022/06/29-183902.85' IN (
  's3://practical-cockroachdb-backups-us-west?AWS_ACCESS_KEY_ID=****&AWS_
SECRET_ACCESS_KEY=****&AWS_REGION=us-west-1&COCKROACH_LOCALITY=default',
  's3://practical-cockroachdb-backups-us-east?AWS_ACCESS_KEY_
ID=****&AWS_SECRET_ACCESS_KEY=****&AWS_REGION=us-east-1&COCKROACH_
LOCALITY=region%3Dus-east-1'
);
```

KMS keys and encryption passphrases can be used in conjunction with regional backups, making for flexible backup and restores with CockroachDB.

Scheduled Backups

It's safe to assume that you won't want to manually back up your cluster at midnight every night. That's where CockroachDB's backup schedules come in. The following statement creates two backup schedules:

- **Weekly full backup** – A weekly full backup is created to ensure a clean baseline backup for each week is captured.

- **Daily incremental backup** – A daily backup is created as per our instructions using crontab syntax.

```
CREATE SCHEDULE cluster_backup
  FOR BACKUP INTO 's3://practical-cockroachdb-backups?AWS_ACCESS_KEY_
ID=****&AWS_SECRET_ACCESS_KEY=****&AWS_REGION=eu-west-2'
    WITH revision_history
    RECURRING '@daily'
    WITH SCHEDULE OPTIONS first_run = 'now';
```

The output of this statement will contain information for two newly created schedules:

- **Weekly full backup:**
  - ID: 742844058827390977
  - Status: ACTIVE

241

- **Daily incremental backup:**

  - ID: 742844058837024769

  - Status: PAUSED: Waiting for initial backup to complete

Once the initial daily backup has finished, its status will go from PAUSED to ACTIVE. This can be seen with a call to SHOW SCHEDULES:

```
$ cockroach sql --url "postgresql://localhost:26260" --insecure \
    --execute "SHOW SCHEDULES" \
    --format records
```

```
-[ RECORD 1 ]
id              | 742844058837024769
label           | cluster_backup
schedule_status | ACTIVE
next_run        | 2022-03-13 00:00:00+00
recurrence      | @weekly

-[ RECORD 3 ]
id              | 742844058827390977
label           | cluster_backup
schedule_status | ACTIVE
next_run        | 2022-03-09 00:00:00+00
recurrence      | @daily
```

Our daily backup job will next execute tomorrow at midnight, whereas our weekly backup job will next execute on Sunday.

We asked CockroachDB to start our first daily backup immediately. This will unlikely be your desired behavior if creating the schedule in the middle of the day. To set a different time for the first run to start, simply replace the first_run value with a timestamp. For example:

```
CREATE SCHEDULE cluster_backup
  FOR BACKUP INTO 's3://practical-cockroachdb-backups?AWS_ACCESS_KEY_
ID=****&AWS_SECRET_ACCESS_KEY=****&AWS_REGION=eu-west-2'
    WITH revision_history
    RECURRING '@daily'
    WITH SCHEDULE OPTIONS first_run = '2022-03-08 00:00:00+00';
```

Cluster Design

When designing your cluster, there are numerous configurations you'll need to decide between to get optimal performance and resilience. In this section, we'll focus on these decisions and their trade-offs.

Cluster Sizing

If you think about your CockroachDB cluster as a collection of vCPUs (Virtual CPUs) that are distributed across nodes, the process of architecting your cluster becomes simpler.

There are trade-offs between having a cluster with a small number of large nodes and a cluster with a large number of smaller nodes.

In a small cluster of large nodes, the additional computing power of each machine and fewer network hops required to satisfy large queries make for a more **stable** cluster.

In a large cluster of small nodes, the additional nodes to distribute data and parallelize distributed operations like backups and restores make for a more **resilient** cluster.

The decision between stability and resilience is yours to make, but as a rule-of-thumb, Cockroach Labs recommends that you meet in the middle and distribute your vCPUs across as few nodes as possible while still achieving resilience. Their Production Checklist[12] offers a detailed breakdown of each scenario.

Node Sizing

Cockroach Labs provides a simple set of recommendations for sizing your cluster nodes based on their vCPU count. Let's go through each of the recommendations against the minimum and recommended vCPU counts. Note that these are just general recommendations. Depending on your unique performance requirements, you may require different ratios:

- **Memory** – 4GB per vCPU:

    - 4 vCPUs -> 16GB of RAM per node

    - 8 vCPUs -> 32GB of RAM per node

---

[12]www.cockroachlabs.com/docs/stable/recommended-production-settings.html

- **Storage** – 150GB per vCPU:

  - 4 vCPUs -> 600GB of disk per node

  - 8 vCPUs -> 1.2TB of disk per node

- **IOPS** – 500 IOPS (input/output operations per second) per vCPU:

  - 4 vCPUs -> 2,000 IOPS

  - 8 vCPUs -> 4,000 IOPS

- **MB/s** – 30MB/s (amount of data transferred to or from disk per second) per vCPU:

  - 4 vCPUs -> 120MB/s

  - 8 vCPUs -> 240MB/s

It's often said that "premature optimization is the root of all evil." The same applies when creating the architecture your CockroachDB cluster will live in. Back in 2018, I was creating a CockroachDB cluster and asked the Cockroach Labs team whether they recommended immediately placing an external cache in front of my CockroachDB cluster to cater for read-heavy workloads. Their response was to start by harnessing CockroachDB's own cache. This would result in fewer network hops and would provide query atomicity, whereas a combination of database and cache would not.

With CockroachDB, you have the freedom to not only scale the number of nodes in your cluster but also the nodes themselves. So design to support a sensible initial capacity and grow from there.

Monitoring

An important aspect of running any software safely in production is monitoring. In this section, we'll configure monitoring for a CockroachDB cluster and raise alerts against a simple metric.

For this example, we'll use Prometheus, a popular open source monitoring system that CockroachDB has great support for.

First, we'll create a cluster to monitor:

```
$ cockroach start \
  --insecure \
  --store=node1 \
  --listen-addr=localhost:26257 \
  --http-addr=localhost:8080 \
  --join=localhost:26257,localhost:26258,localhost:26259

$ cockroach start \
  --insecure \
  --store=node2 \
  --listen-addr=localhost:26258 \
  --http-addr=localhost:8081 \
  --join=localhost:26257,localhost:26258,localhost:26259

$ cockroach start \
  --insecure \
  --store=node3 \
  --listen-addr=localhost:26259 \
  --http-addr=localhost:8082 \
  --join=localhost:26257,localhost:26258,localhost:26259

$ cockroach init --insecure --host=localhost:26257
```

Next, we'll create an instance of Prometheus to monitor our three nodes. We'll create prometheus.yml and alert_rules.yml configuration files and point the Prometheus instance at those.

The prometheus.yml file configures the basic properties of Prometheus. It dictates how frequently Prometheus will scrape for metrics, which hosts to scrape metrics from, and which URLs those hosts are serving metrics on. Note that because I'll be running Prometheus using Docker, I use the host.docker.internal DNS name, which resolves out of the container to my host machine:

```
global:
  scrape_interval: 10s

rule_files:
  - alert_rules.yml
```

```
scrape_configs:
  - job_name: cockroachdb
    metrics_path: /_status/vars
    static_configs:
      - targets:
        - host.docker.internal:8080
        - host.docker.internal:8081
        - host.docker.internal:8082
```

The alert_rules.yml file configures alert groups containing metric rules. If any metric rules breach configured thresholds, an alert will be raised for that group. For this example, I create an alert that will fire if CockroachDB detects that a node has been offline for one minute:

```
groups:
- name: node_down
  rules:
  - alert: NodeDown
    expr: up == 0
    for: 1m
    labels:
      severity: critical
```

Next, we'll create an instance of Alertmanager. This will receive alerts from Prometheus and direct them to a receiver. With the following configuration, I use a simple HTTP receiver to send notifications to https://httpbin.org:

```
global:
  resolve_timeout: 5m

route:
  group_by: ['alertname']
  group_wait: 5s
  group_interval: 5s
  repeat_interval: 1h
  receiver: api_notify
```

```
receivers:
  - name: api_notify
    webhook_configs:
      - url: https://httpbin.org/post
```

Let's start Prometheus and Alertmanager now:

```
$ docker run \
    --name prometheus \
    --rm -it \
    -p 9090:9090 \
    -v ${PWD}/prometheus.yml:/etc/prometheus/prometheus.yml \
    -v ${PWD}/alert_rules.yml:/etc/prometheus/alert_rules.yml \
    prom/prometheus
```

```
$ docker run \
    --name alertmanager \
    --rm -it \
    -p 9093:9093 \
    -v ${PWD}/alertmanager.yml:/etc/alertmanager/alertmanager.yml \
    prom/alertmanager
```

If you visit http://localhost:9090/alerts, you'll see that the NodeDown alert is active and reporting that no nodes are currently down:

```
∨ NodeDown (0 active)
name: NodeDown
expr: up == 0
for: 1m
labels:
    severity: critical
```

If we kill a node now, the alert will enter a "pending" state before "firing." I'll terminate the cockroach process for node3 to demonstrate these alert statuses.

After a short while, the alert will enter the pending state:

⌄ NodeDown (1 active)

```
name: NodeDown
expr: up == 0
for: 1m
labels:
   severity: critical
```

Labels	State	Active Since	Value
alertname=NodeDown instance=host.docker.internal:8082 job=cockroachdb severity=critical	PENDING	2022-06-30T06:55:51.956992479Z	0

After a little longer, it will enter the firing state:

⌄ NodeDown (1 active)

```
name: NodeDown
expr: up == 0
for: 1m
labels:
   severity: critical
```

Labels	State	Active Since	Value
alertname=NodeDown instance=host.docker.internal:8082 job=cockroachdb severity=critical	FIRING	2022-06-30T06:55:51.956992479Z	0

If we restart node3 and wait a short while, the alert will clear and report that our cluster is once again healthy.

Index

A

Antipatterns, 152–156
argPlaceholders, 212
Availability zones (AZs), 21, 140, 141, 151

B

Backing up and restoring data
    backups with revision history, 231
    encrypted backups, 231, 237–240
    full backups, 231, 233–235
    incremental backups, 231, 236
    locality-aware backups, 232
    scheduled backups, 241, 242
Backup methods, 232
Backups with revision history, 231–232
Basic Production topology, 140, 141, 160
Bean About Town, 161
Black Box testing
    API server listening, 173
    application, 166
    application, testing, 173
    database's internal structure, 165
    error handling, 174
    GET request handler, 167, 169, 172
    malformatted customer ID, 176
    mechanism, 166
    multistatement transaction, 176
    POST request endpoint, 168
    POST request handler, 167
    Product class, 168
    request for nonexistent ID, 176

serialization, 170
testing with application code, 179–184

C

The California Consumer Privacy Act
    (CCPA), 124, 126–128
Certificate Authority (CA), 70, 130
Change Data Capture (CDC), 6, 114, 116,
    119, 120, 156
Changefeeds, 116
Cloud provider blob storage, 232
Cluster design
    cluster sizing, 243
    node sizing, 243, 244
Cluster maintenance
    cluster-wide operations, 220
    Frankfurt cluster, 223
    gossip protocol, 221
    Kubernetes users, 225
    node start command, 220
    scaling, 221, 222
Cockroach binary, 67
    cockroach cert command, 70, 71
    command tree, 68
    demo commands, 69
    import command, 78
    node command, 73–76
    recommission command, 77
    sample databases, 69, 70
    sqlfmt command, 78, 79
    start and start-single-node
        commands, 68, 69